Mel Bay Presents

Tommy Emmanuel cgp
Frank Vignola

Just Between Frets

transcribed by Vinny Raniolo

as performed by
Tommy Emmanuel cgp
and Frank Vignola

1 2 3 4 5 6 7 8 9 0

© 2010 BY MEL BAY PUBLICATIONS, INC., PACIFIC, MO 63069.
ALL RIGHTS RESERVED. INTERNATIONAL COPYRIGHT SECURED. B.M.I. MADE AND PRINTED IN U.S.A.
No part of this publication may be reproduced in whole or in part, or stored in a retrieval system, or transmitted in any form
or by any means, electronic, mechanical, photocopy, recording, or otherwise, without written permission of the publisher.

Visit us on the Web at www.melbay.com — E-mail us at email@melbay.com

Contents

Songs	Page Number
Tenderly	3
Clouds	9
How High the Moon	18
I've Got a Crush on You/Young at Heart	35
Swing 39/Swing 42	43
Sweet Dreams	64
Paper Moon	69
Django's Castle	91
Swing 09	101
Nature Boy	111
Just Us 4 All	118

CD on Sollid Air Records….. *www.SolidAirRecords.com*

Available through……. *www.AcousticMusicResource.com*

From *"Torch Song"*. Lyrics by Jack Lawrence. Music by Walter Gross. © 1946, 1947 by Edwin H. Morris & Co. A Division of MPL Music Publishing, Inc. Copyright Renewed, extended term of Copyright deriving from Jack Lawrence assigned and effective August 7, 2002 to Range Road Music Inc. This arrangement © 2010 Edwin H. Morris & Co., A Division of MPL Music Publishing, Inc. All Rights Reserved. Reprinted by permission of Hal Leonard Corporation *(North America)* and Faber o.b.o Warner/Chappell *(World)*

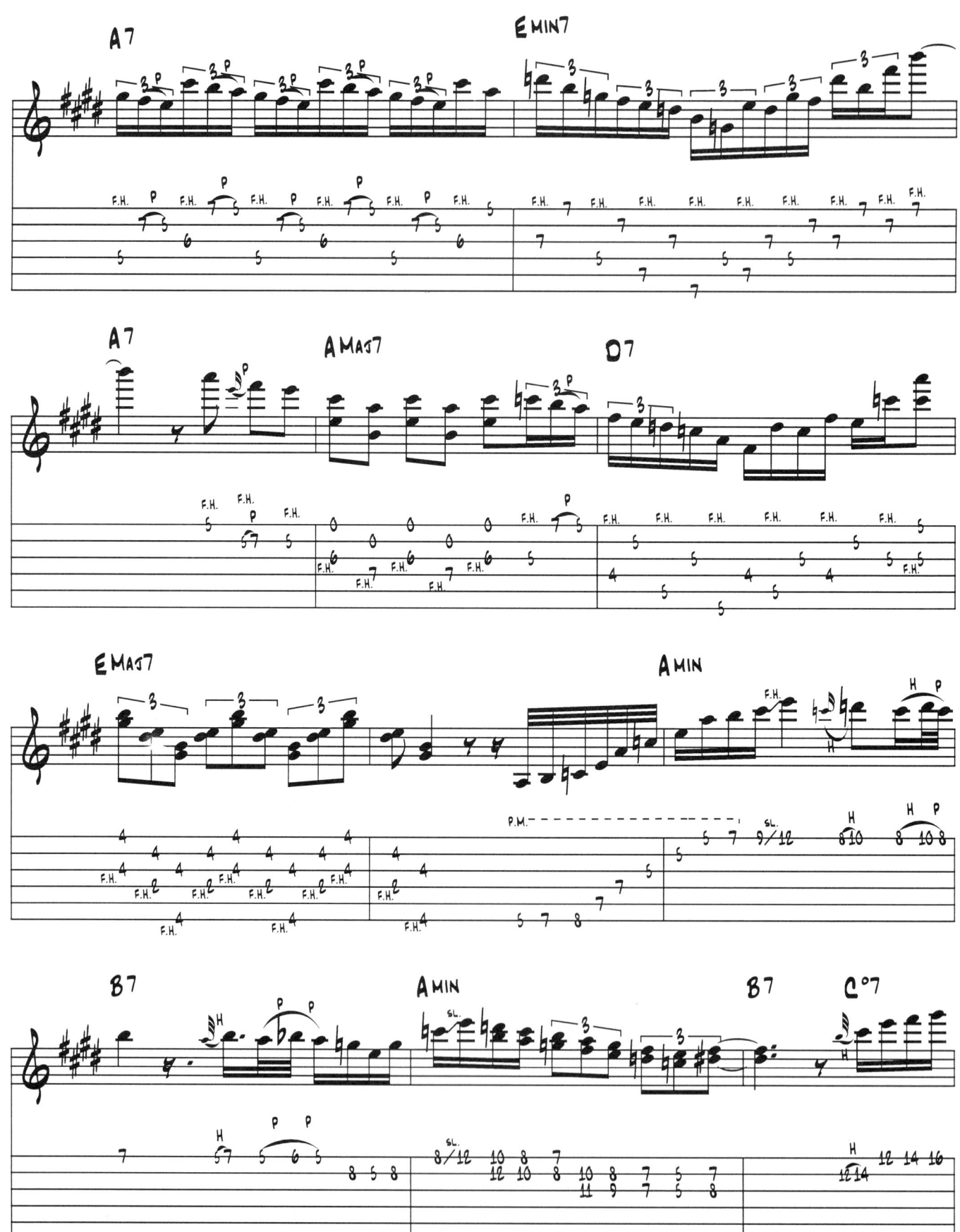

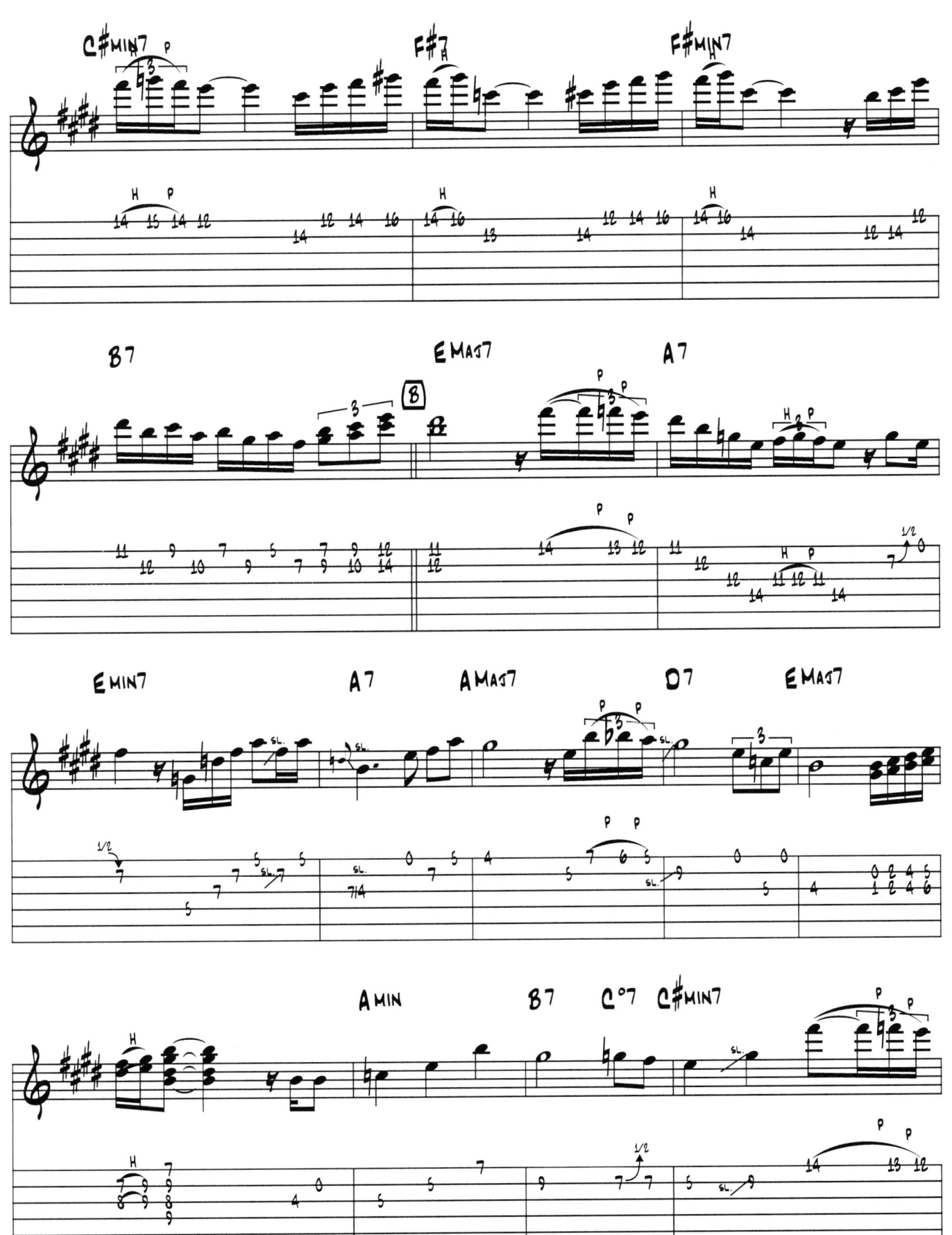

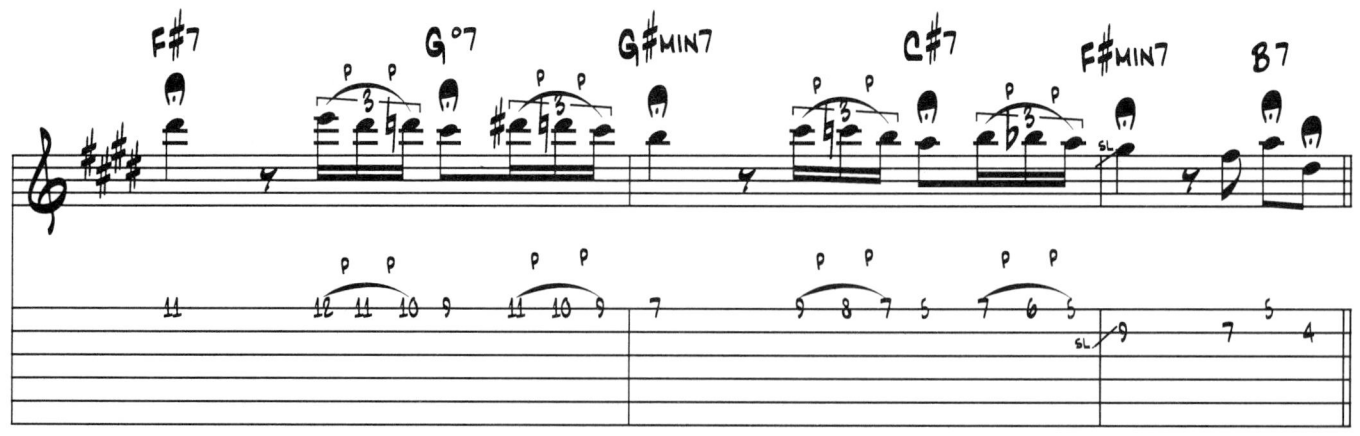

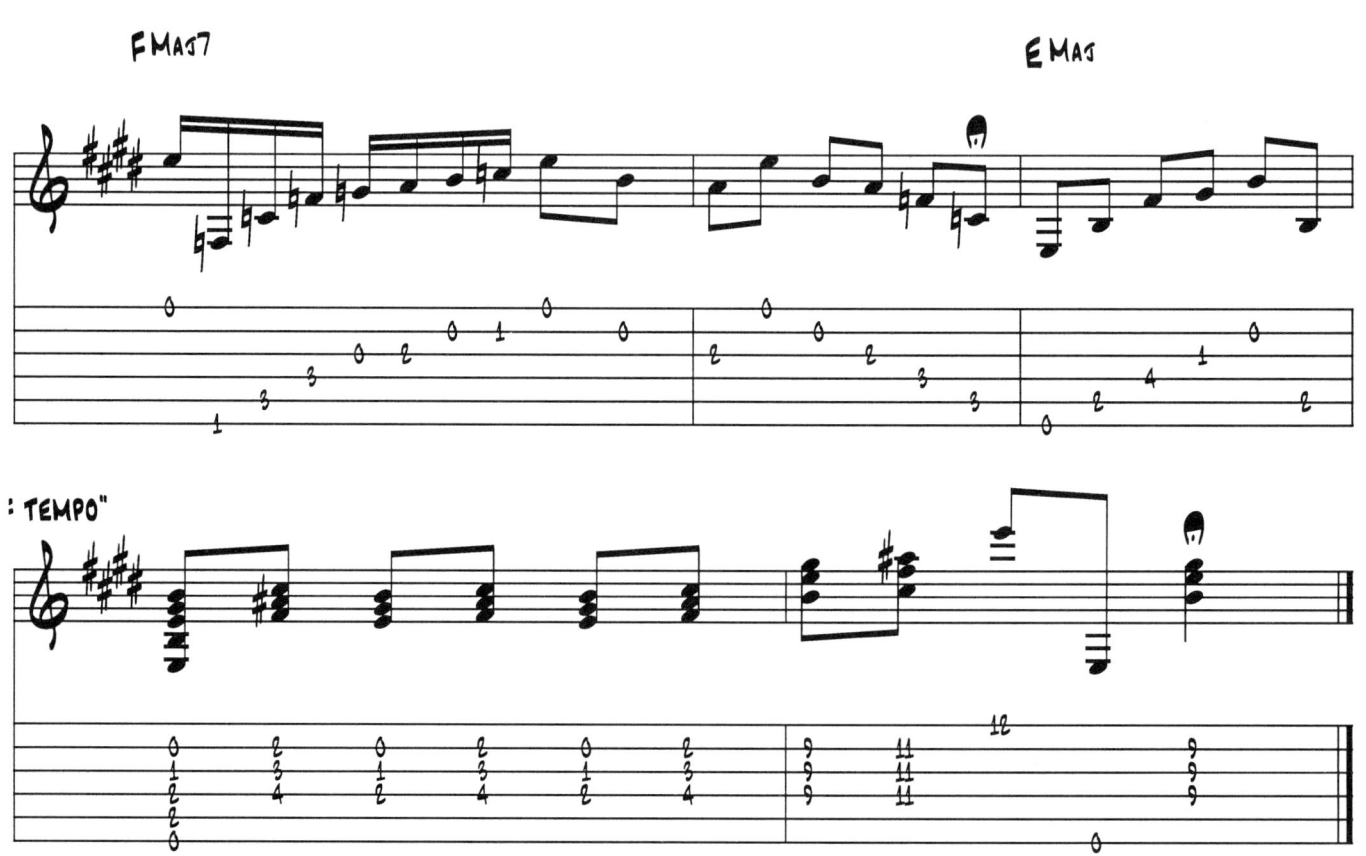

8

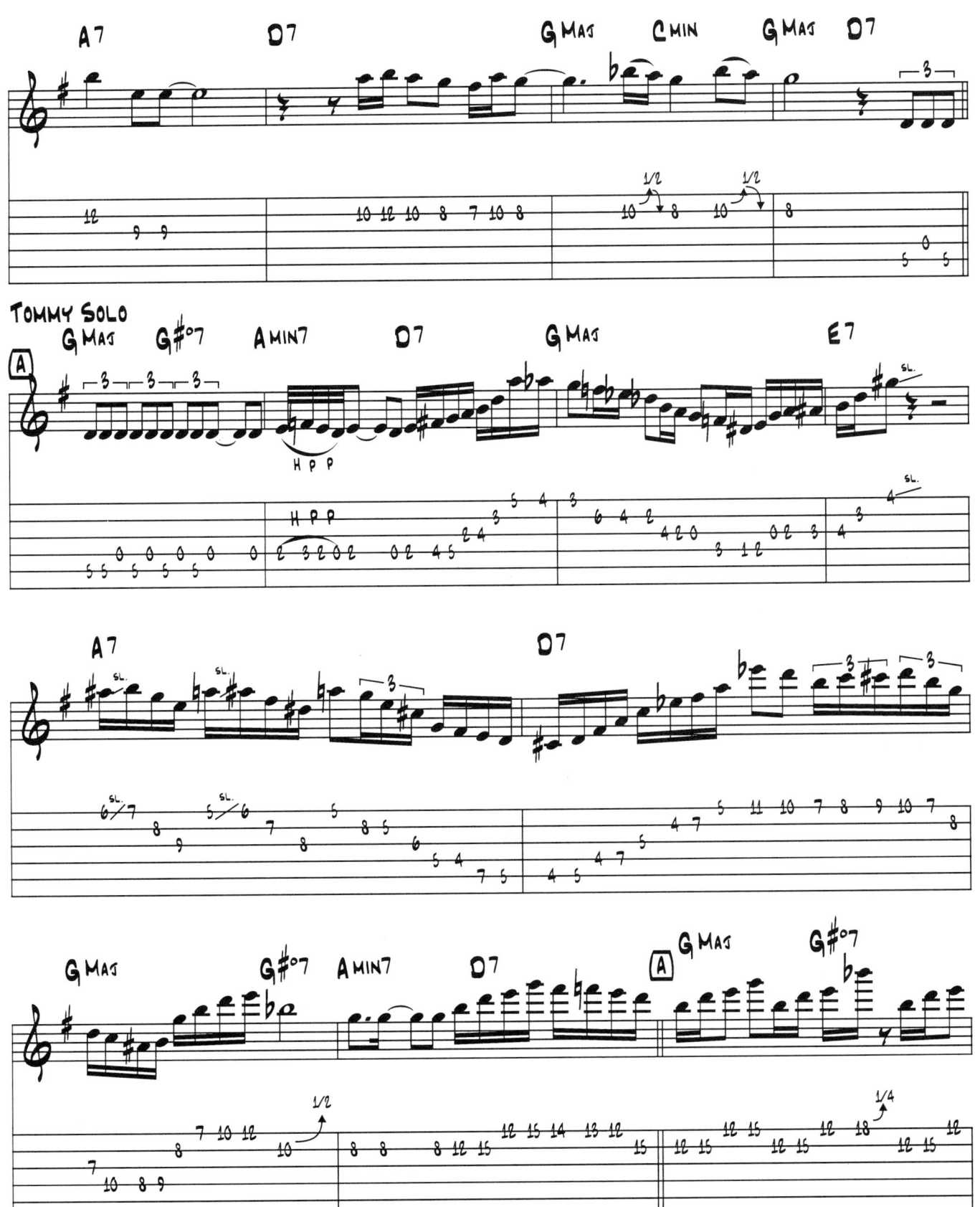

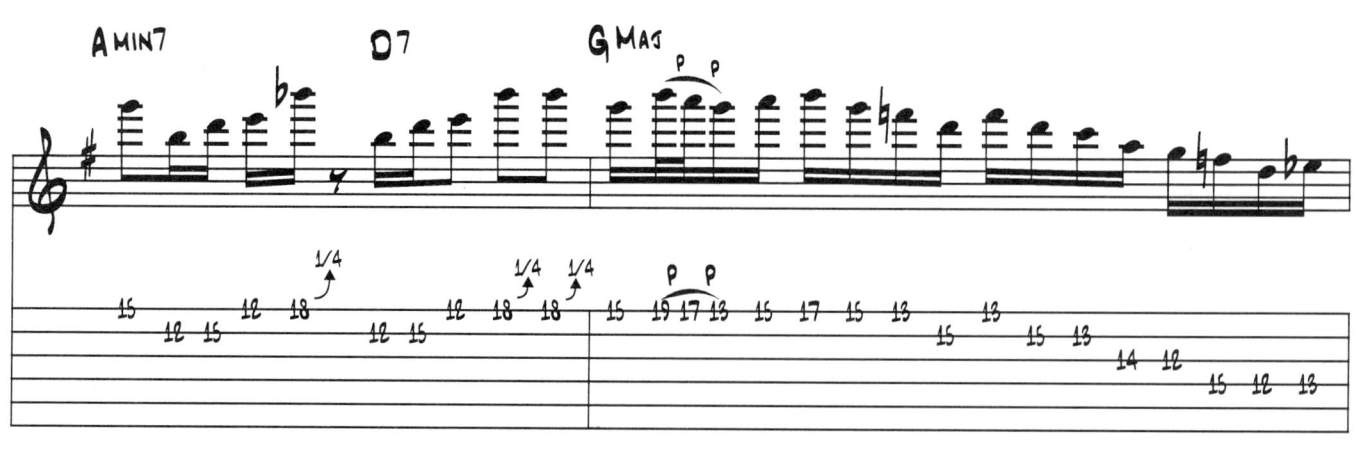

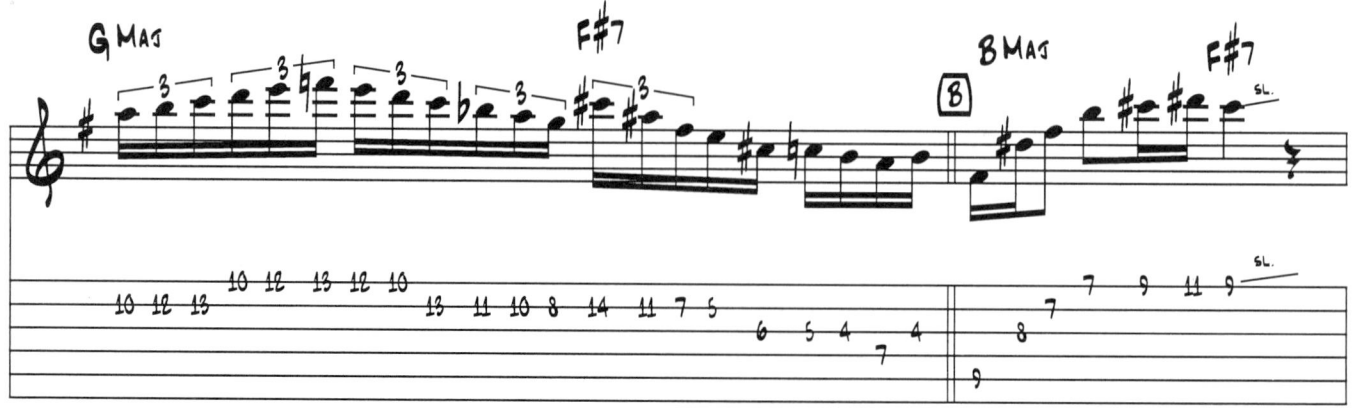

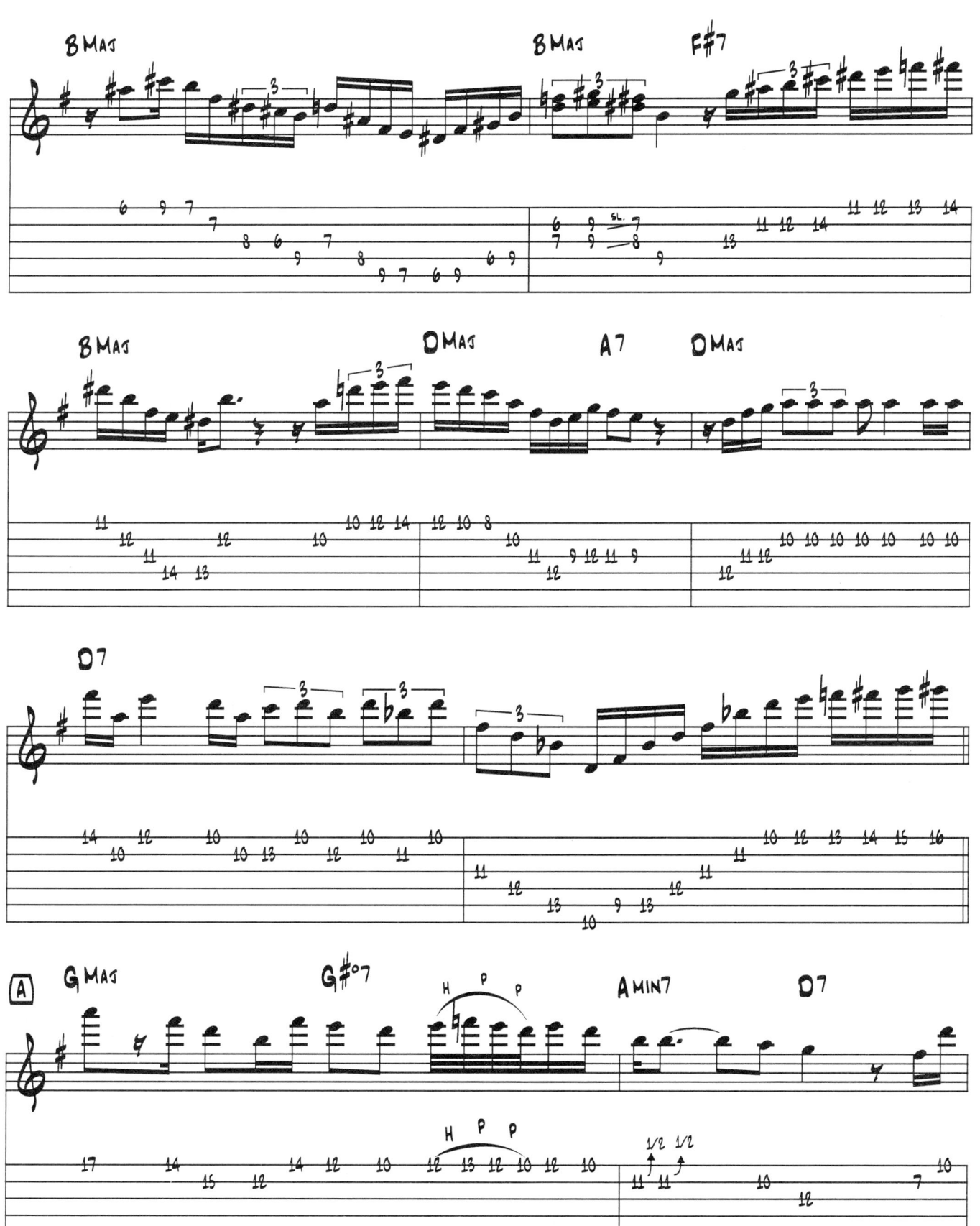

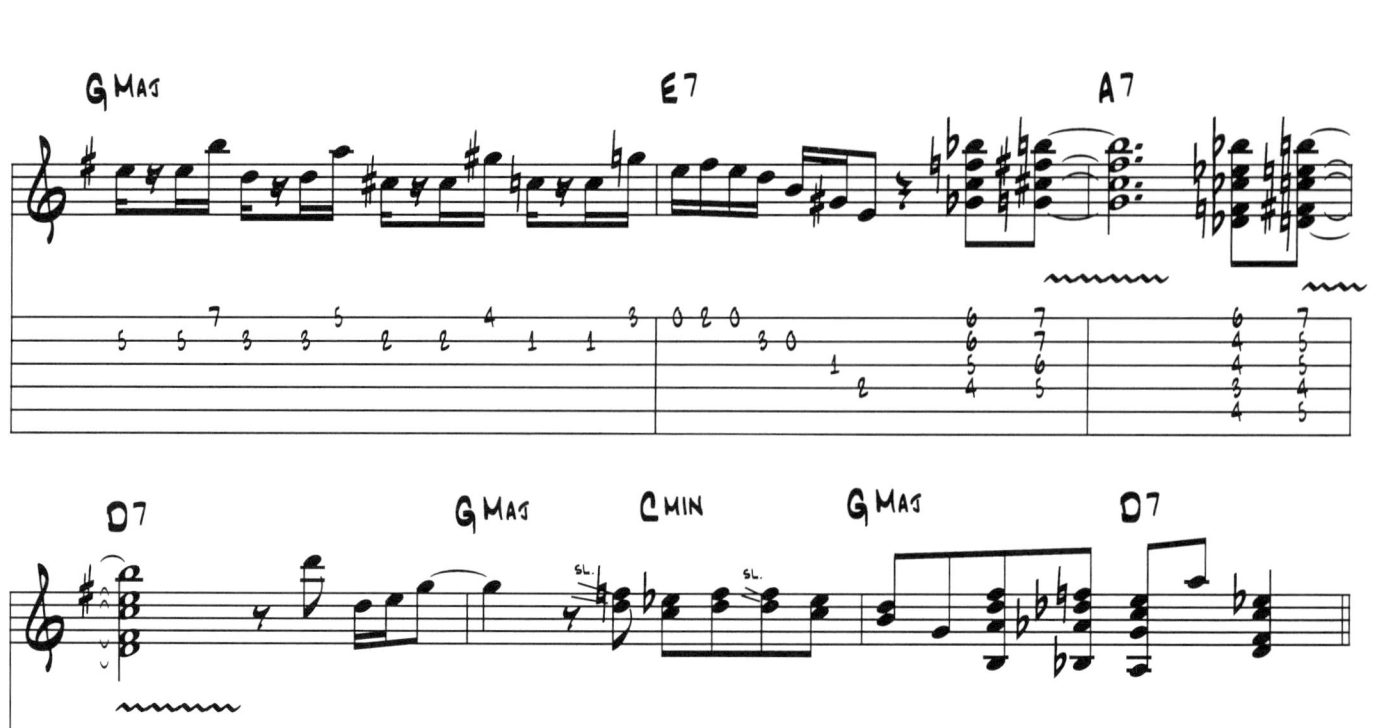

Frank Solo

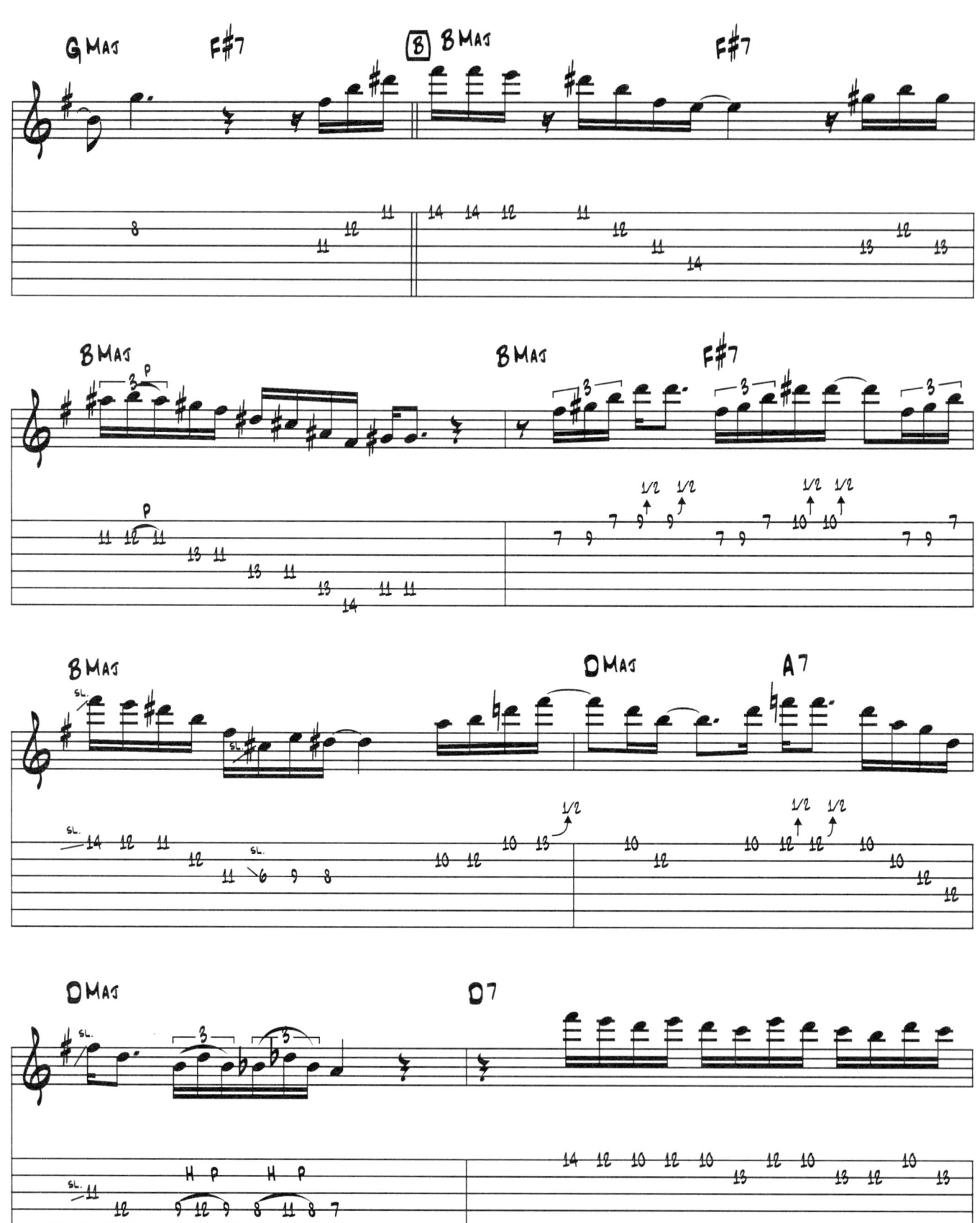

How High The Moon

Intro

From *"Two for the Show"* Words by Nancy Hamilton Music by Morgan Lewis
© 1940 Chappell & Co. Inc. © Renewed. This arrangement © 2010 by Chappell & Co.
International Copyright Secured. All Rights Reserved.
Reprinted by permission of Hal Leonard Corporation *(North America)* and Faber o.b.o Warner/Chappell *(World)*

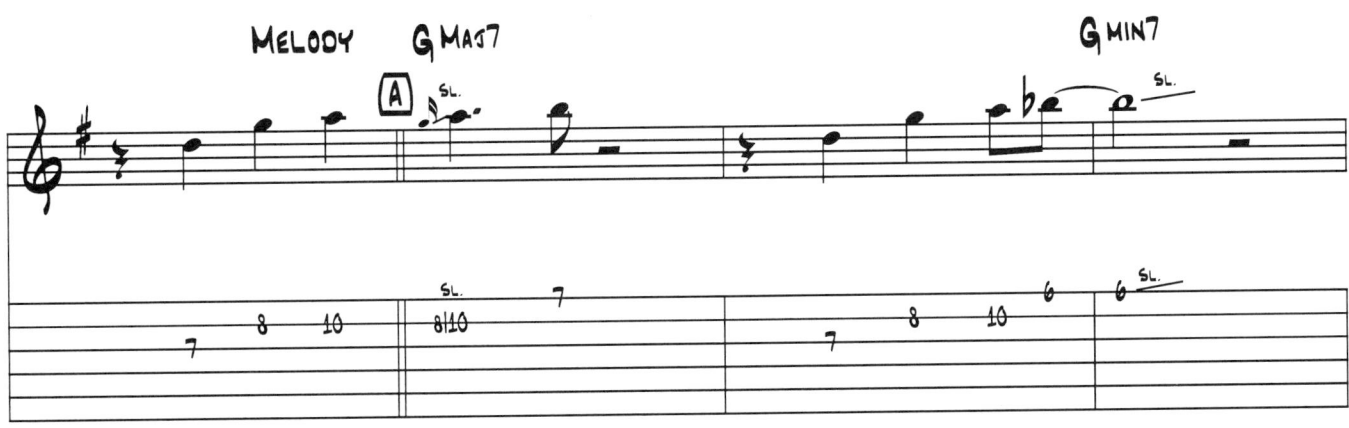

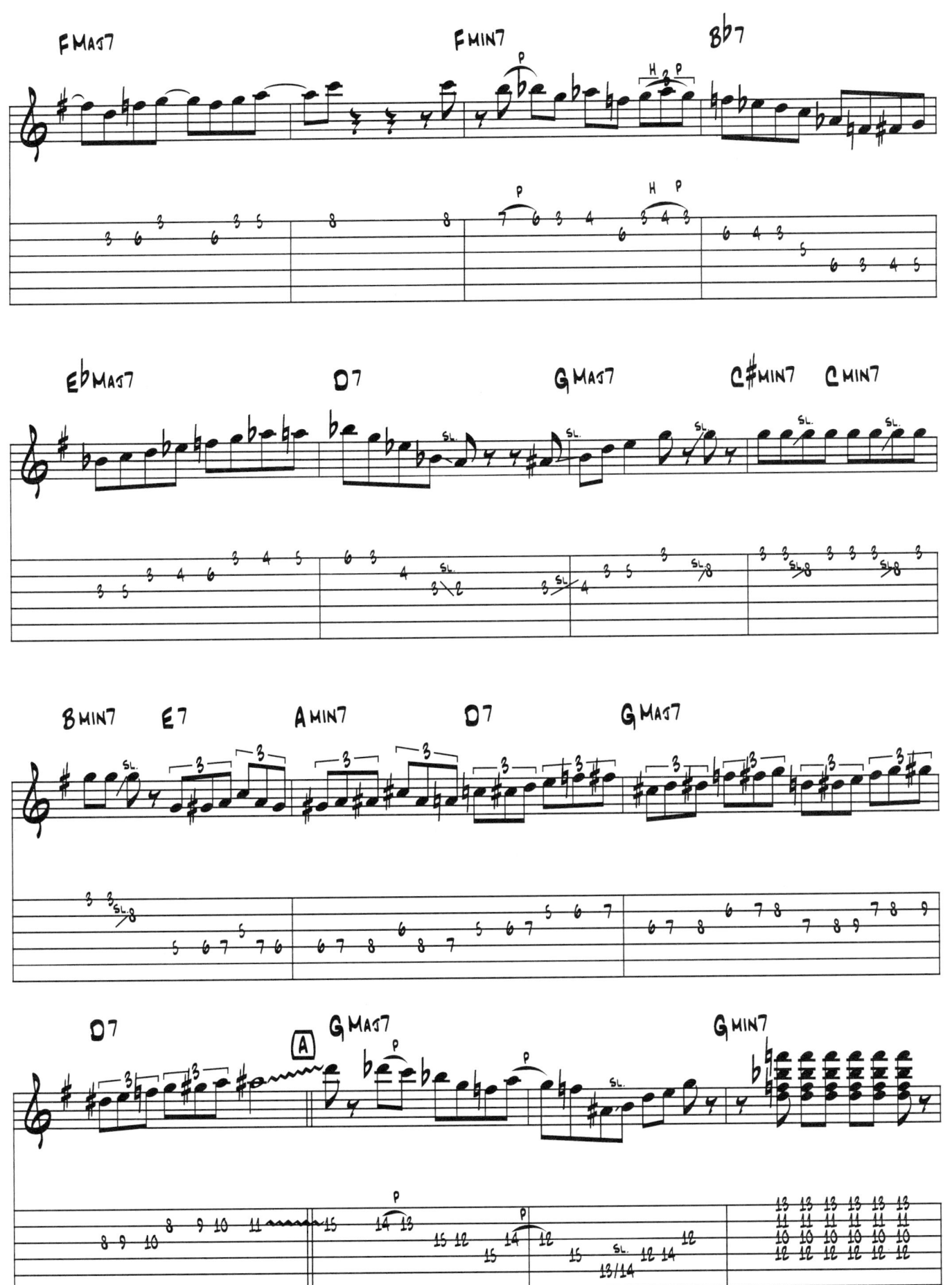

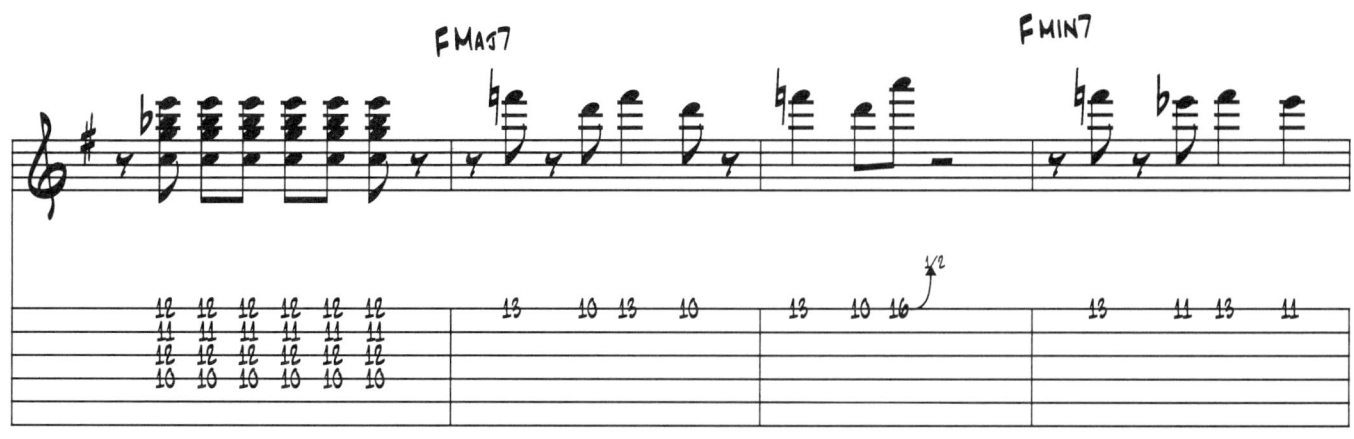

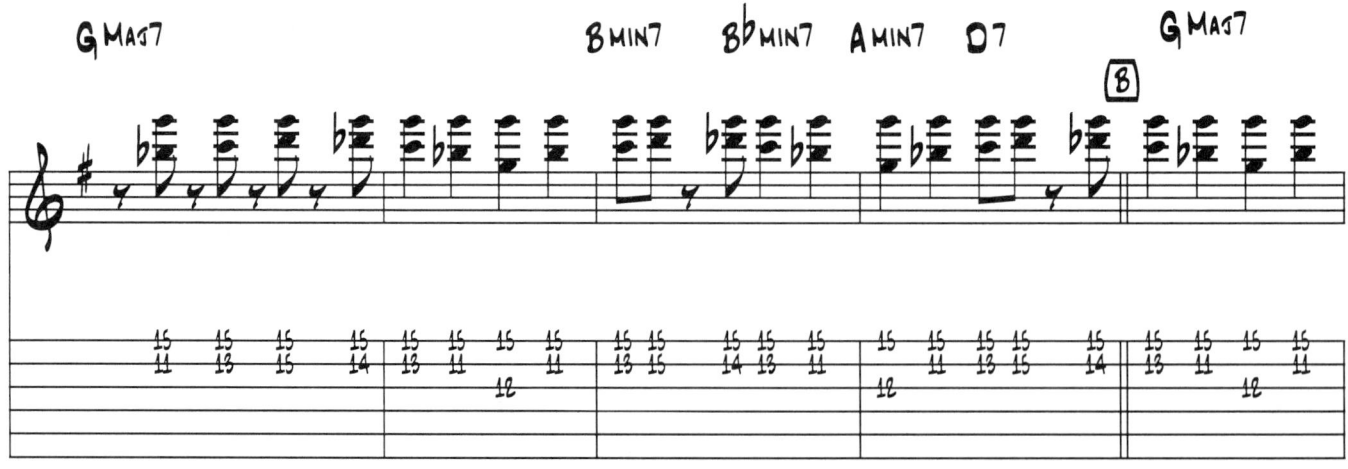

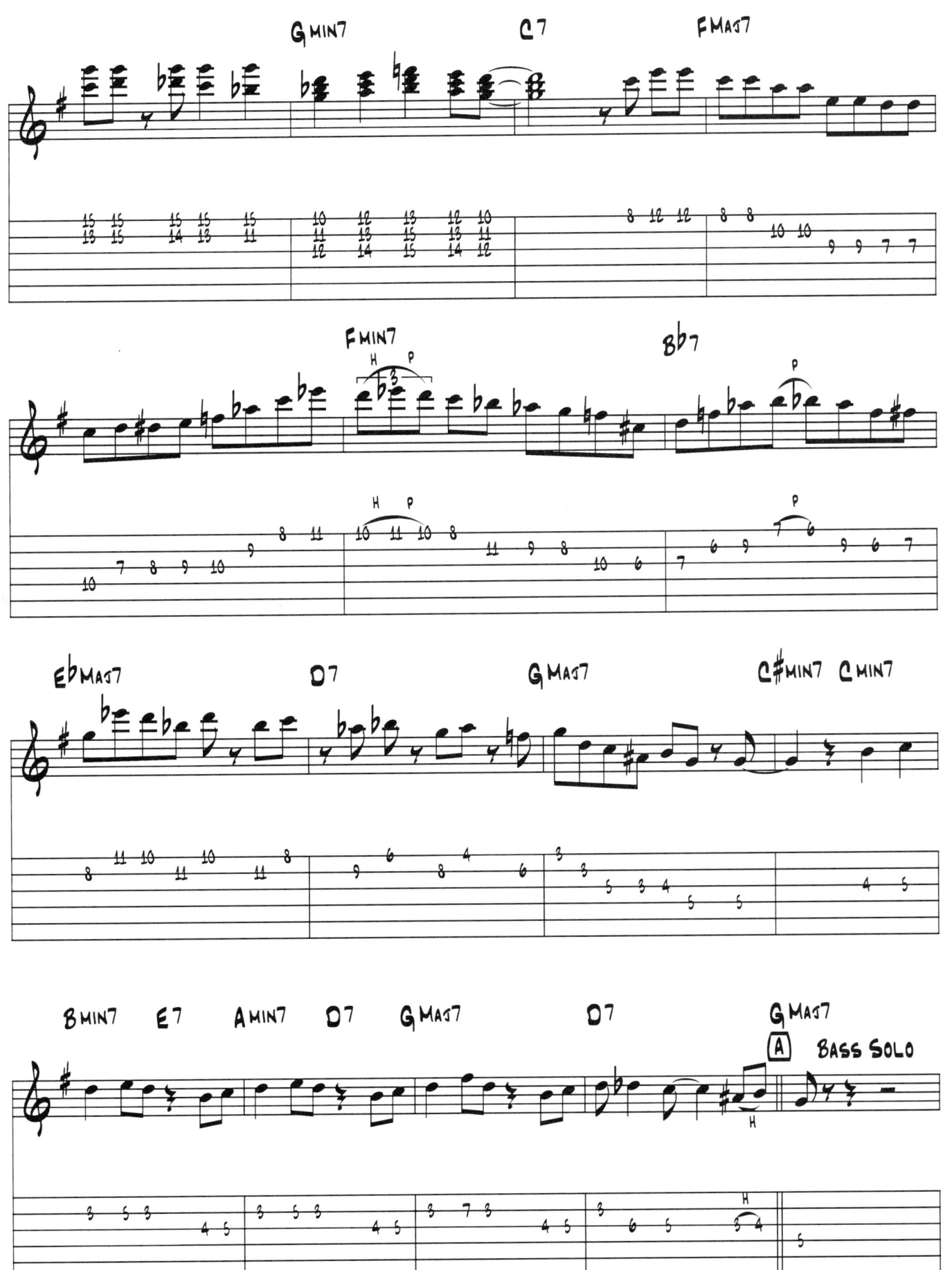

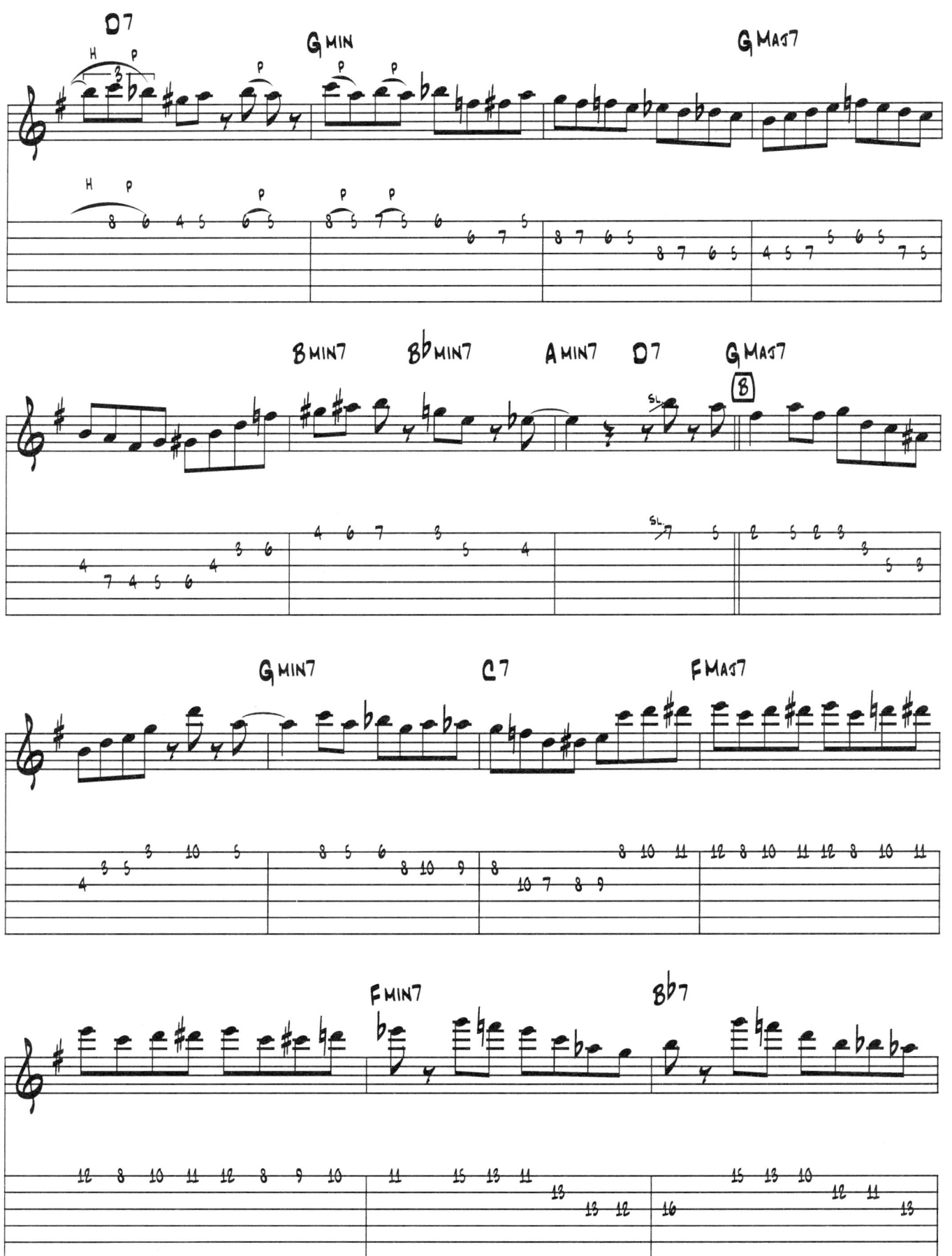

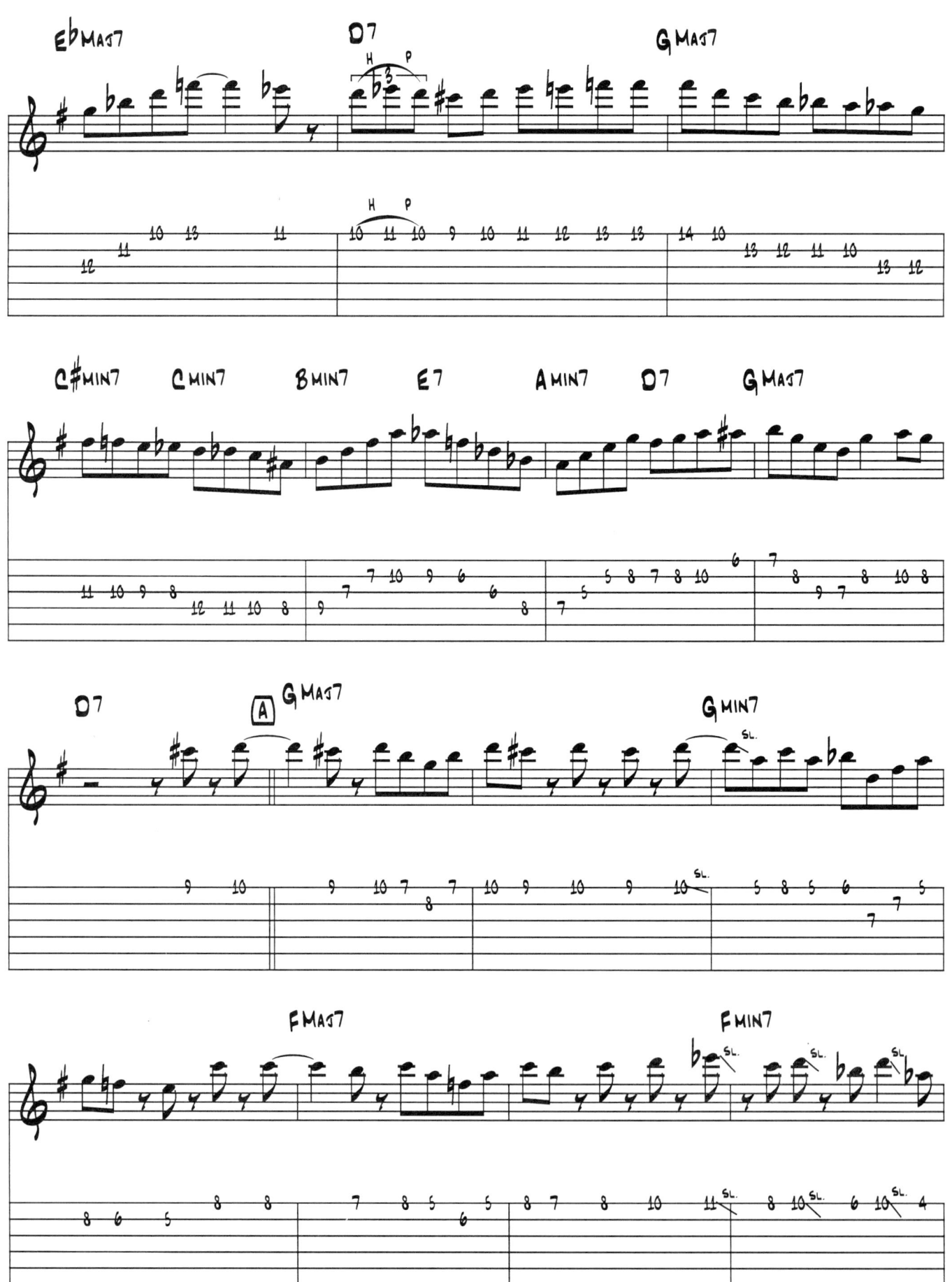

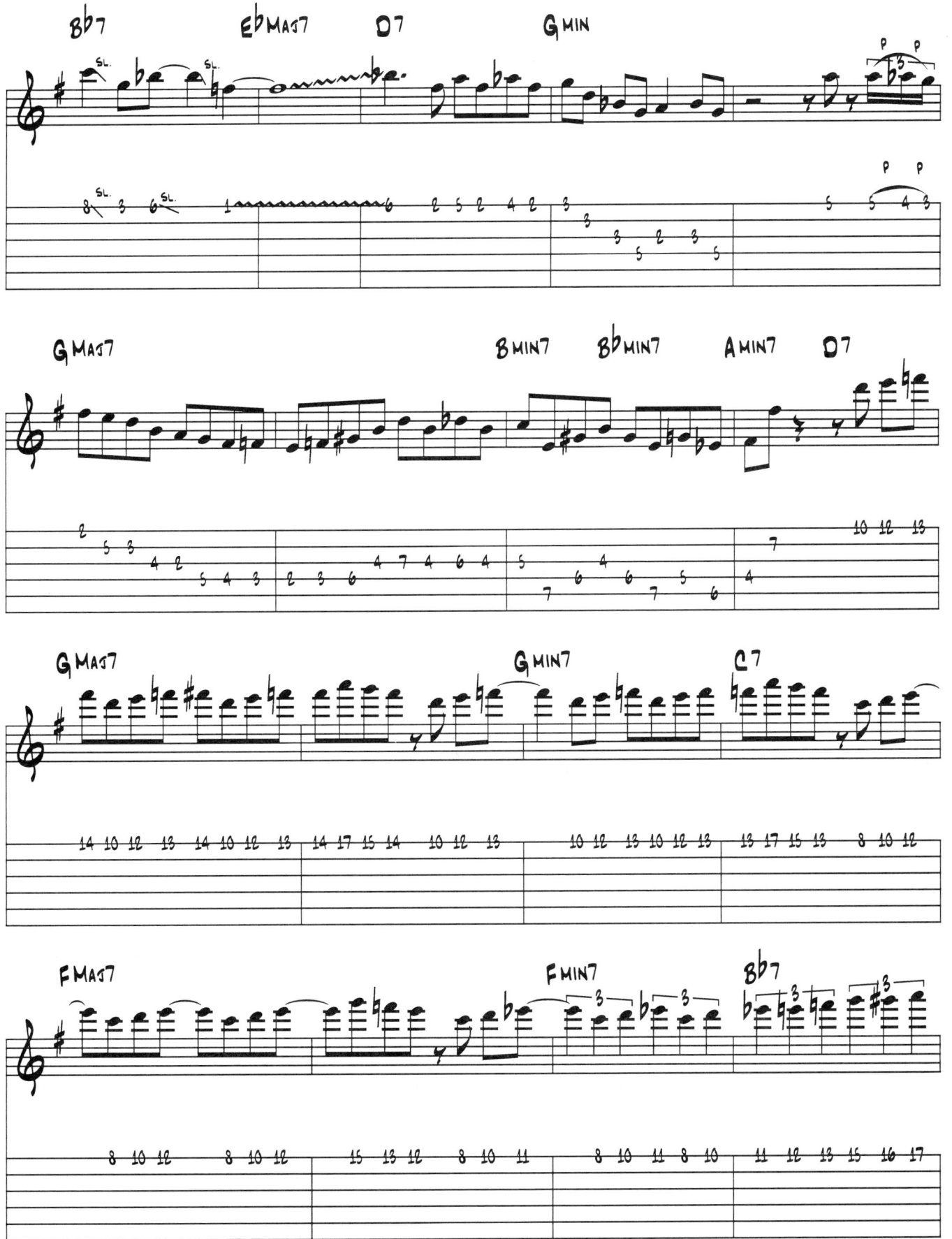

I've Got A Crush On You / Young At Heart

Music and Lyrics by George Gershwin and Ira Gershwin © 1930(Renewed) WB Music Corp. This Arrangement © 2010 WB Music Corp.
All Rights Reserved Including Public Performance.
Used by Permission of Alfred Publishing Co., Inc. *(North America)* and Faber o.b.o. Warner/Chappell *(World)*

Swing 39/Swing 42

Words and Music by Django Reinhardt and Stephane Grappelli © 1939 (Renewed) by Publications Francis Day S. A.
This arrangement © 2010 by Publications Francis Day S.A.
All Rights in the U.S.A. and Canada Controlled by Jewell Music Publishing Co., Inc. (ASCAP)
International Copyright secured. All rights Reserved.
Reprinted by permission of Hal Leonard Corporation *(North America)* and Faber o.b.o. EMI *(World)*

Swing 42 By Django Reinhardt Copyright (c) 1941 (Renewed) by Publications Francis Day S.A. This arrangement Copyright (c) 2010 by Publications Francis Day S.A. All Rights in the U.S.A. and Canada Controlled by Jewel Music Publishing Co., Inc. (ASCAP)
International Copyright Secured   All Rights Reserved   Reprinted by permission of Hal Leonard Corporation

44

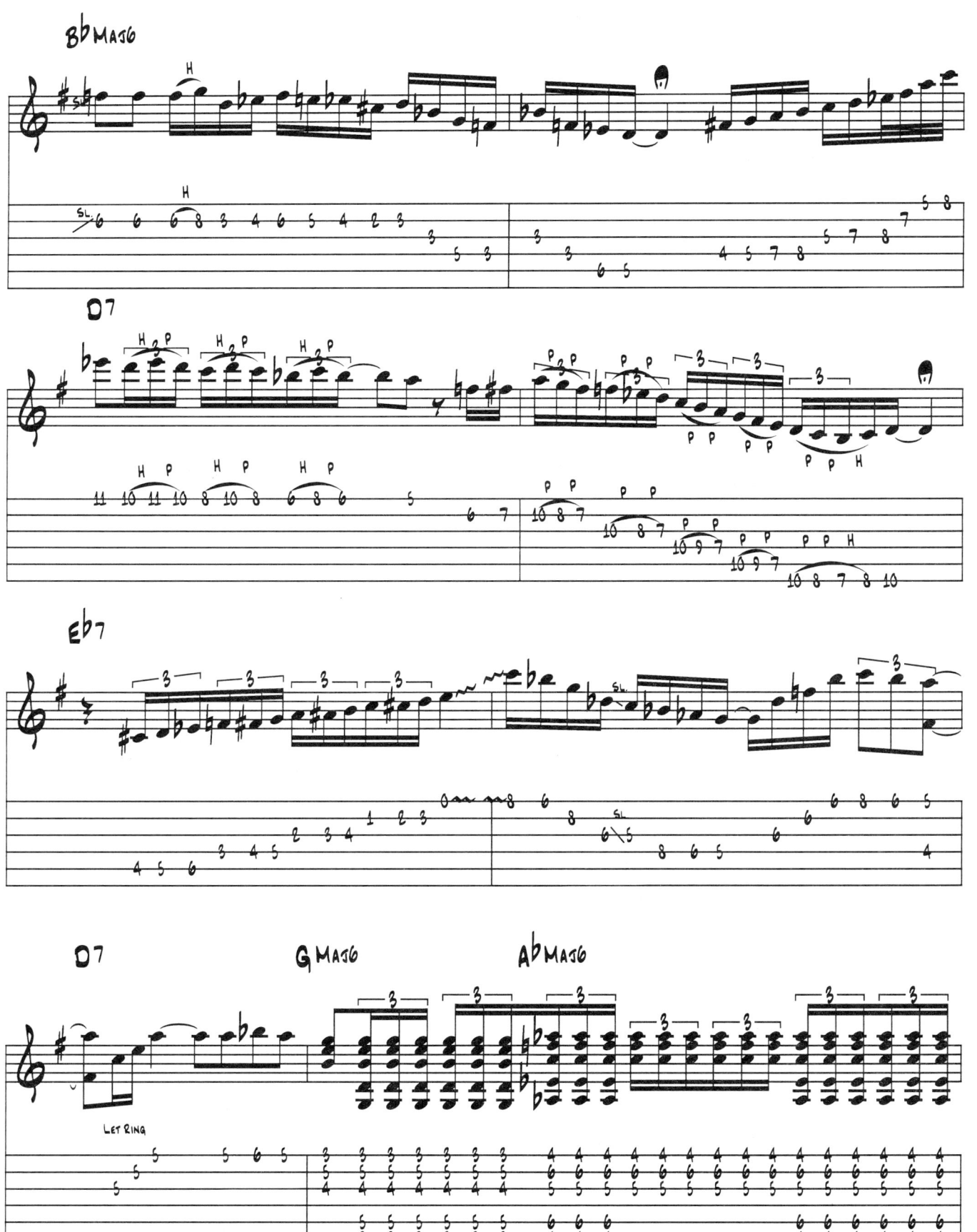

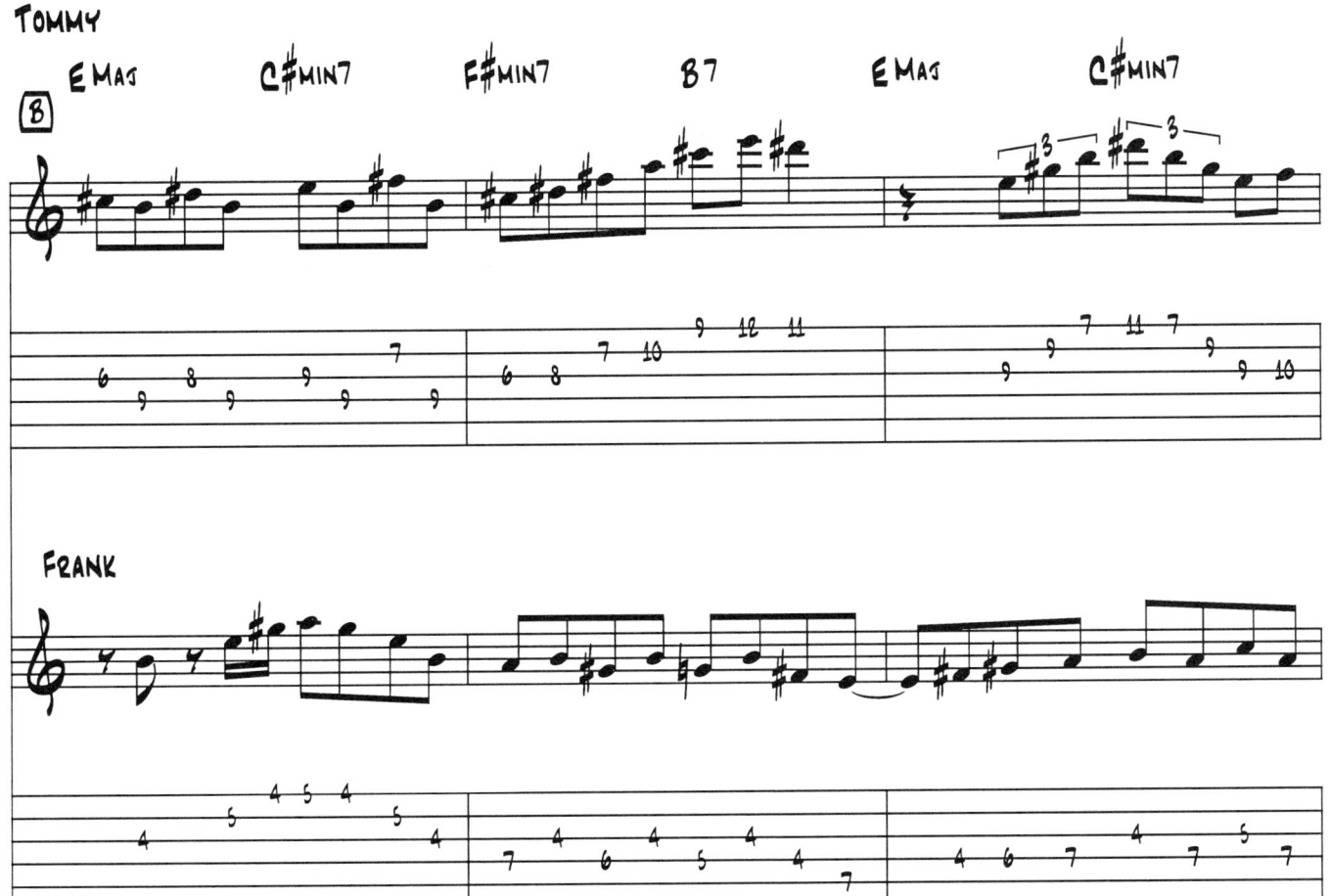

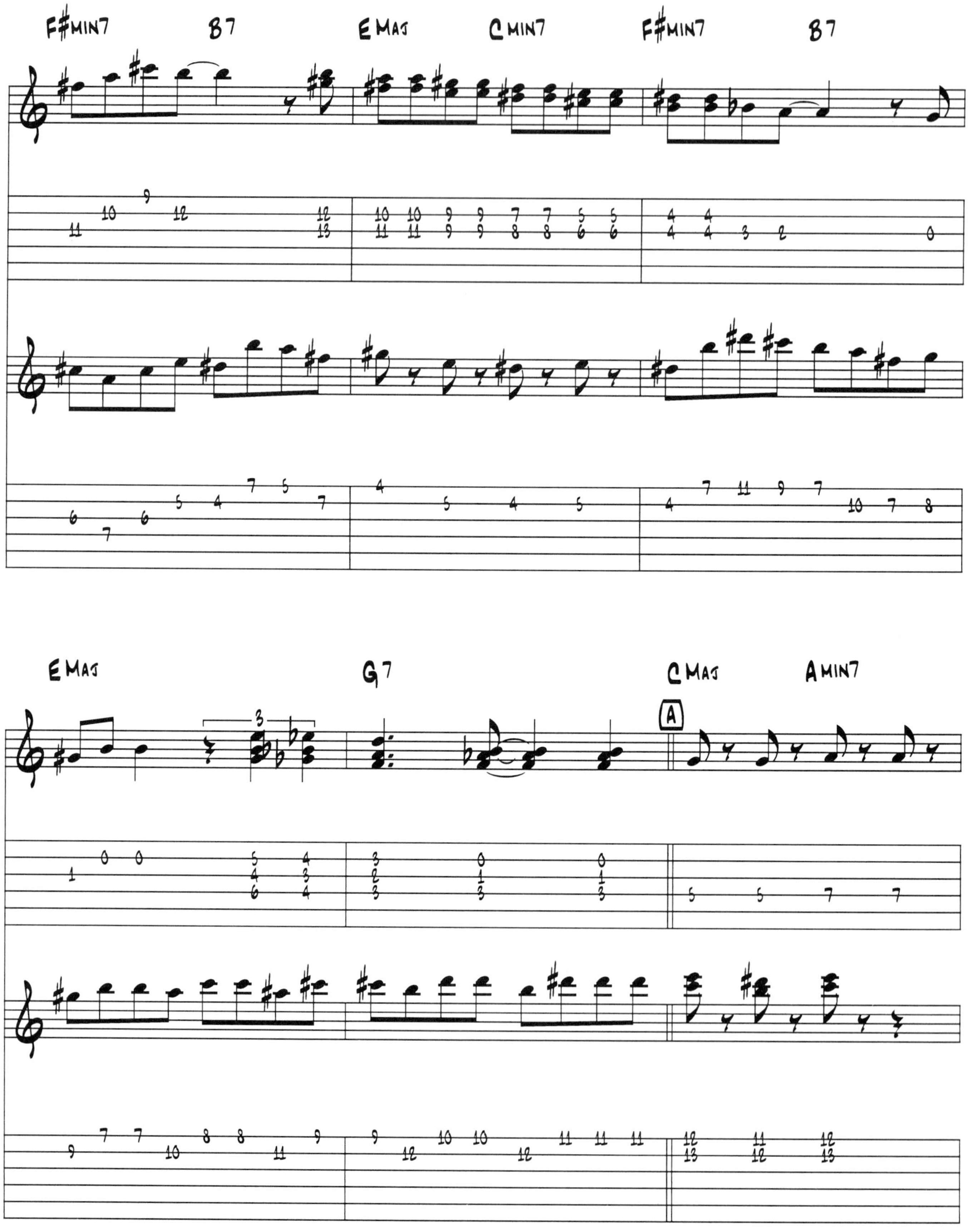
F#MIN7
B7
EMAJ
CMIN7
F#MIN7
B7
EMAJ
G7
CMAJ
AMIN7
A

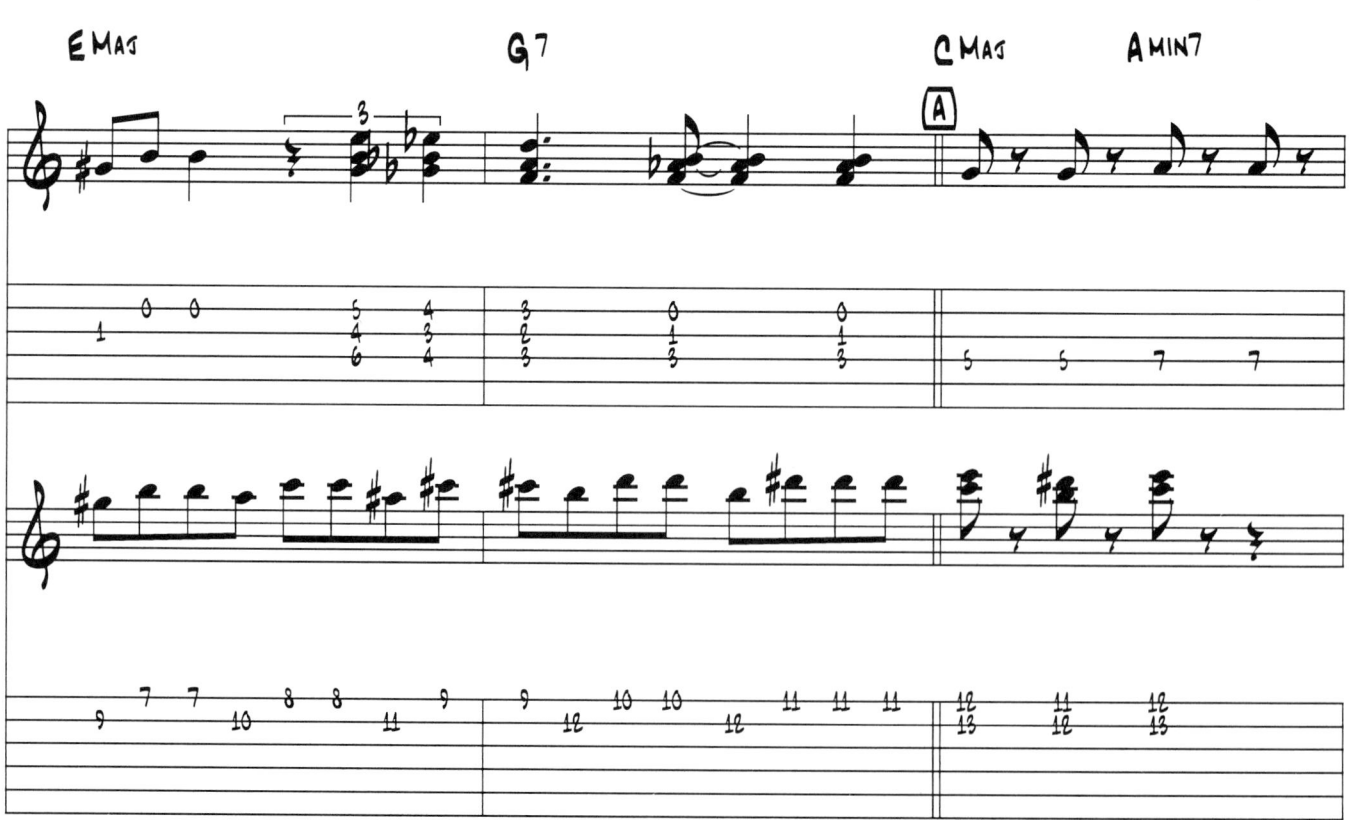

Sweet Dreams

Words and Music by Don Gibson © 1955 Sony/ATV Music Publishing LLC Copyright Renewed
This arrangement © 2010 Sony/ATV Music Publishing LLC
All Rights Administered by Sony/ATV Music Publishing LLC, 8 Music Square West, Nashville, TN 37203
International Copyright Secured. All Rights Reserved.
Reprinted by permission of Hal Leonard Corporation *(North America)* and of Music Sales Limited *(World)*

Paper Moon

Featured in the Motion Picture *"Take a Chance"* Lyrics by Billy Rose and E. Y. "Yip" Harburg Music by Harold Arlen © 1933 (Renewed) Chappell & Co., Glocca Morra Music and S. A. Music Co. This Arrangement © 2010 Chappell & Co., Glocca Morra Music and S. A. Music Co.
All rights for Glocca Morra Music Administered by Next Decade Entertainment, Inc. All Rights Reserved. Used by Permission. Reprinted by permission of Hal Leonard Corporation *(North America)* and of Faber Music *(World)*

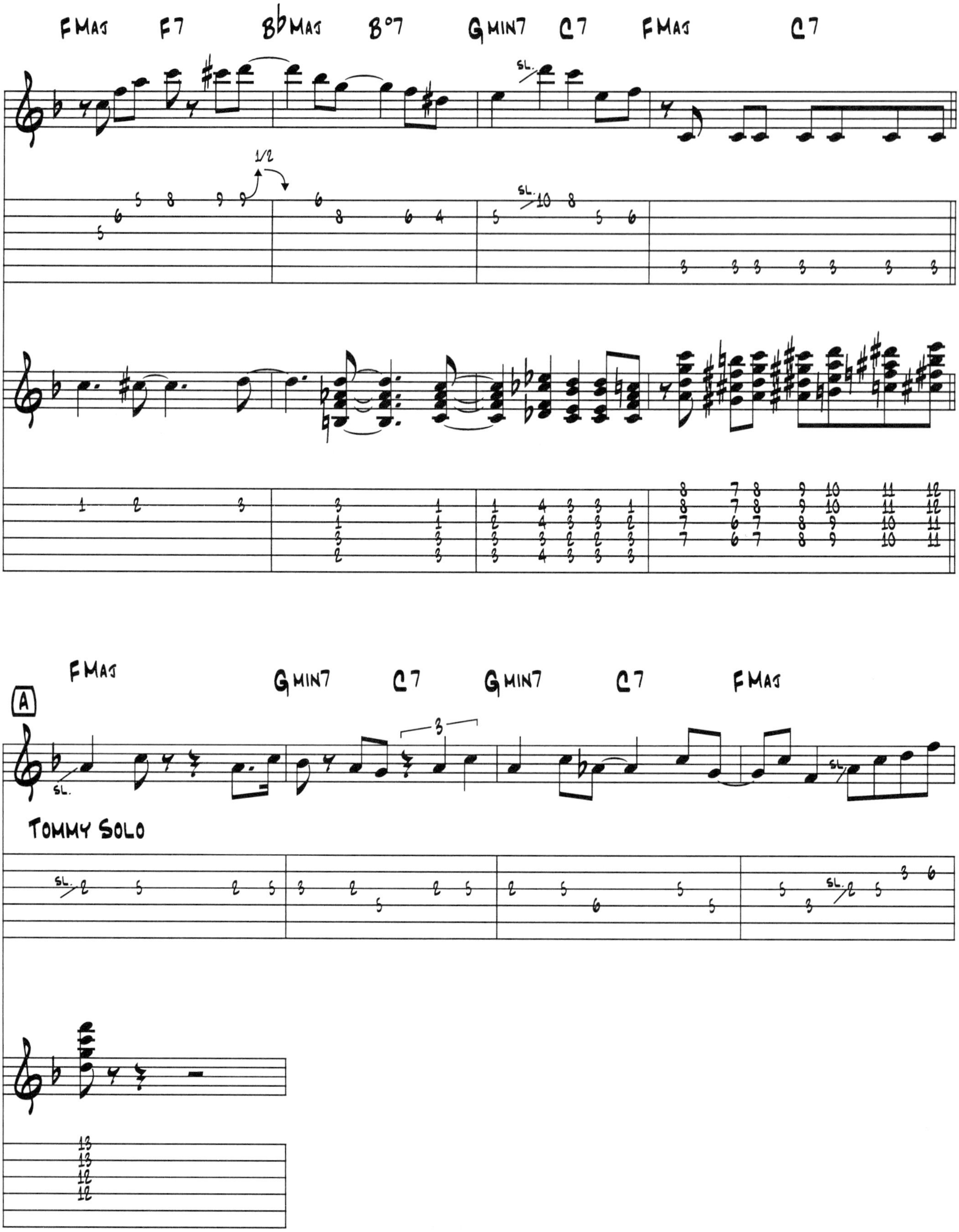
FMAJ F7 B♭MAJ B°7 GMIN7 C7 FMAJ C7
SL.
1/2
SL.
FMAJ GMIN7 C7 GMIN7 C7 FMAJ
A
3
SL.
SL.
TOMMY SOLO
SL.
SL.

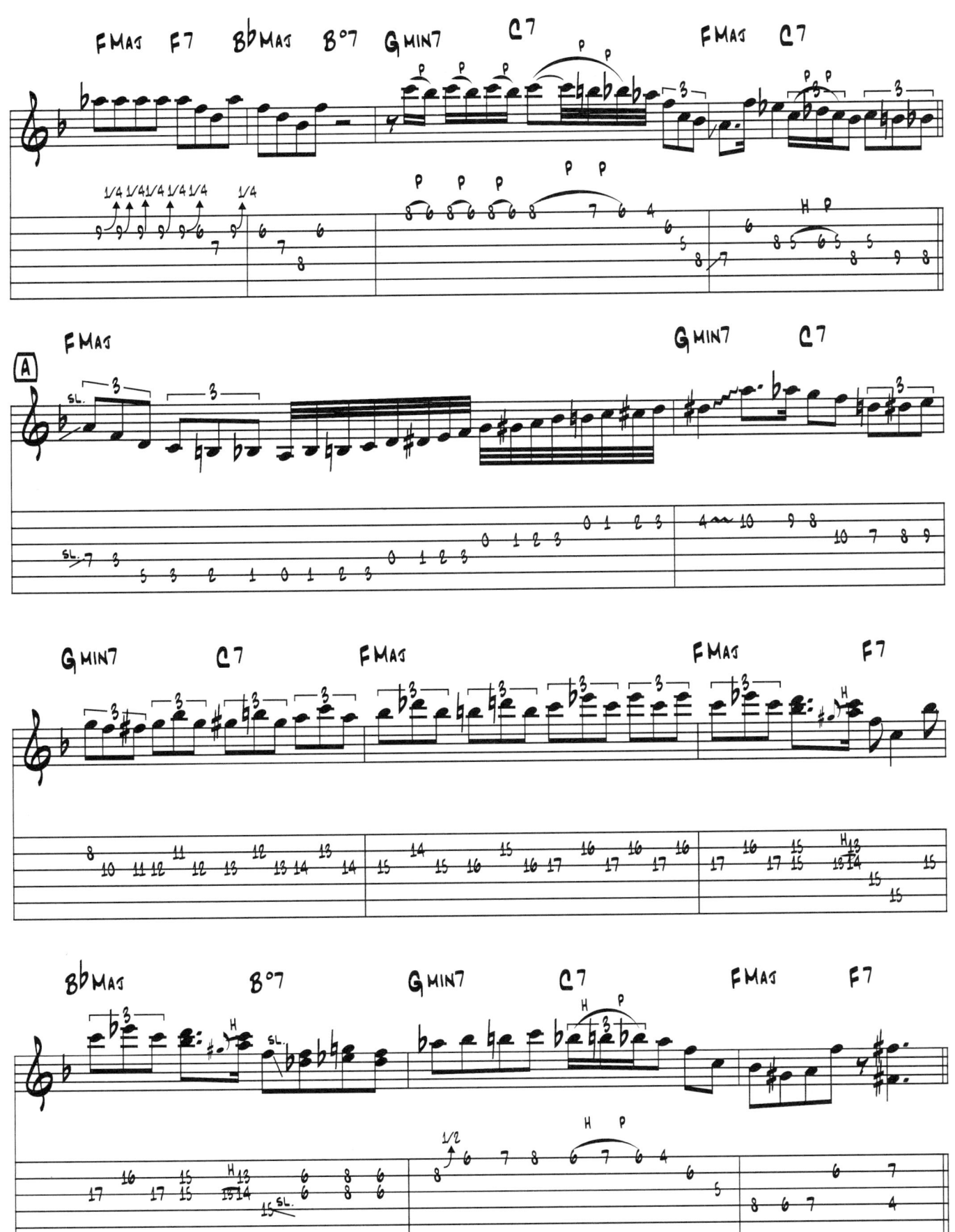

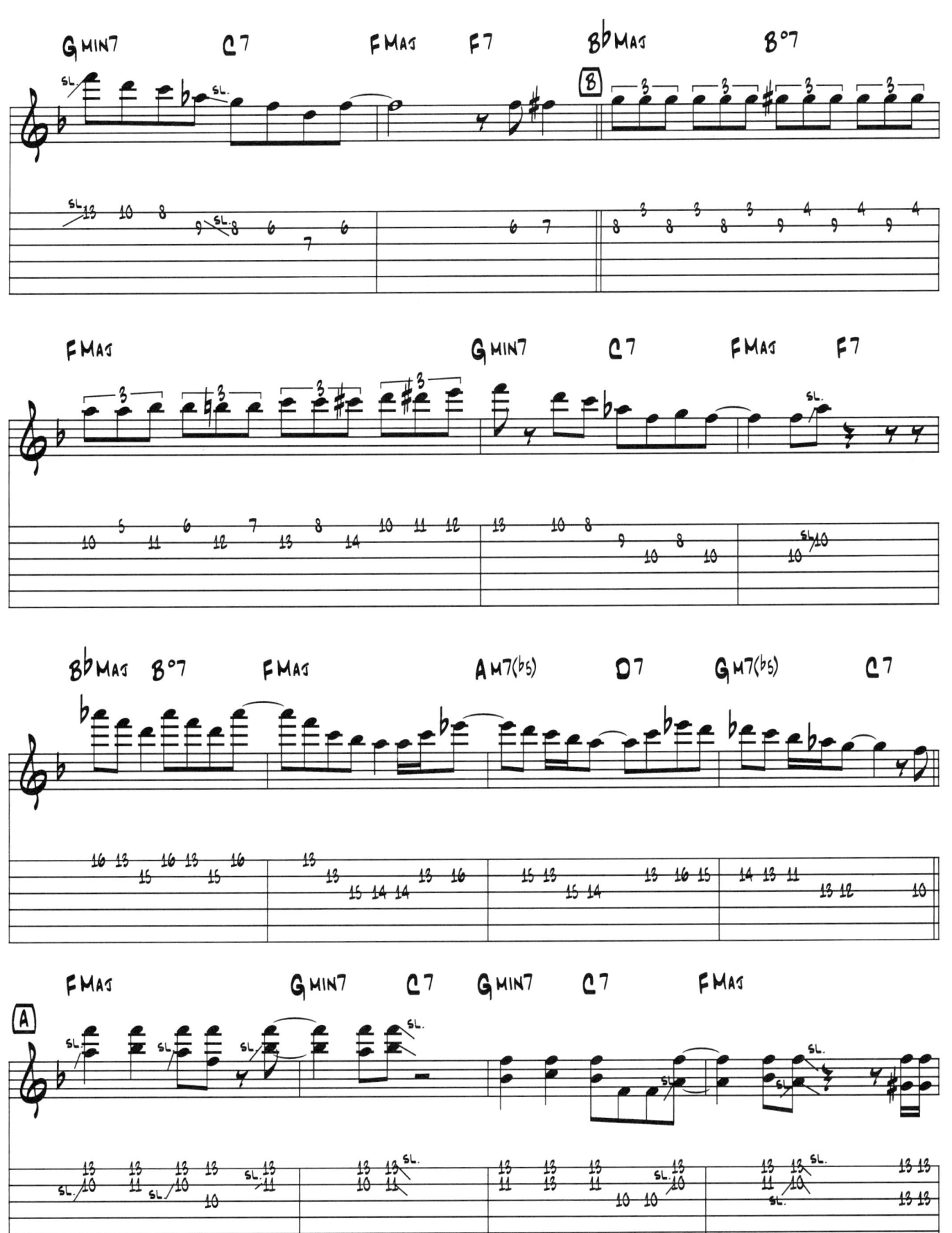

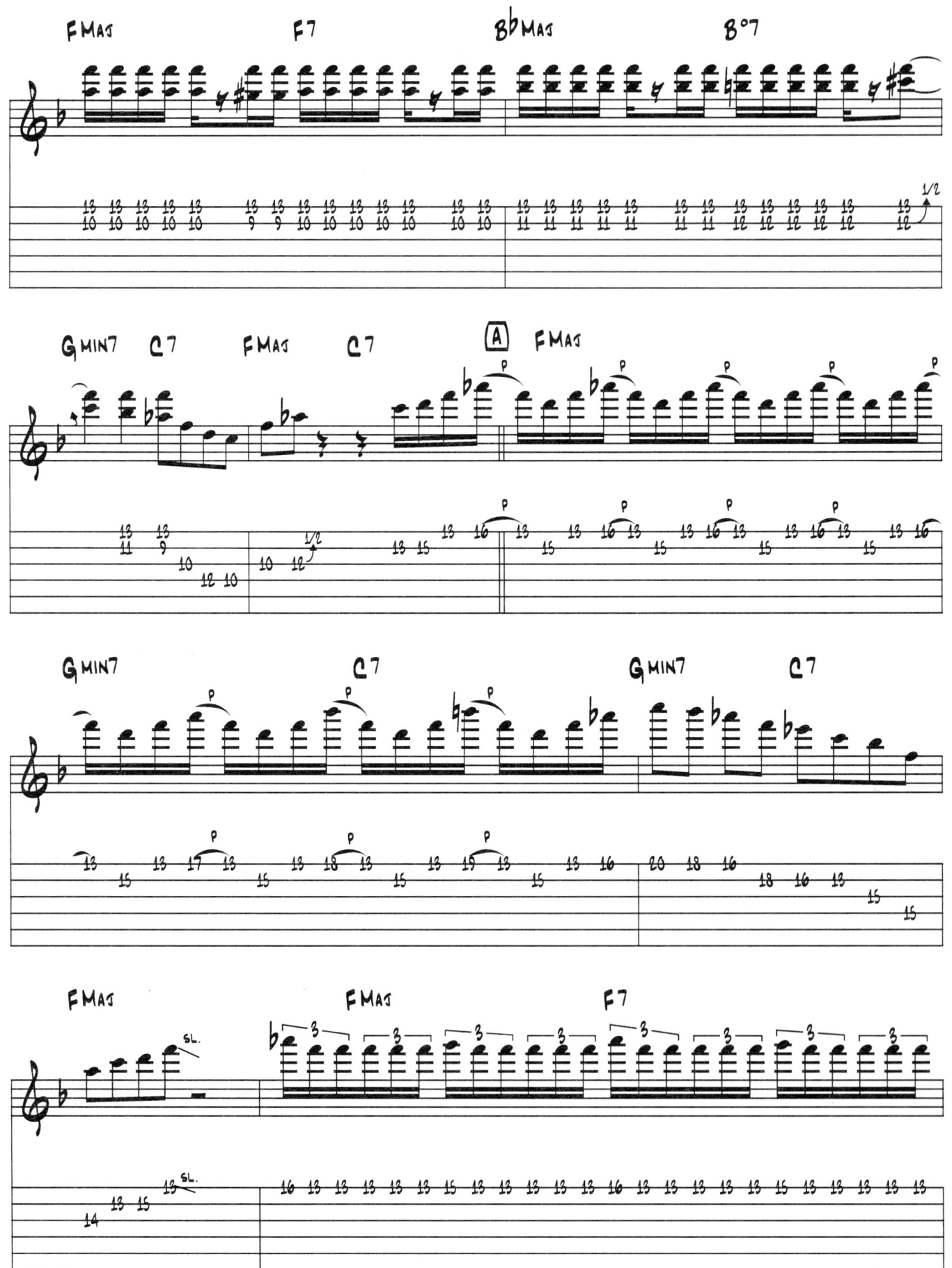

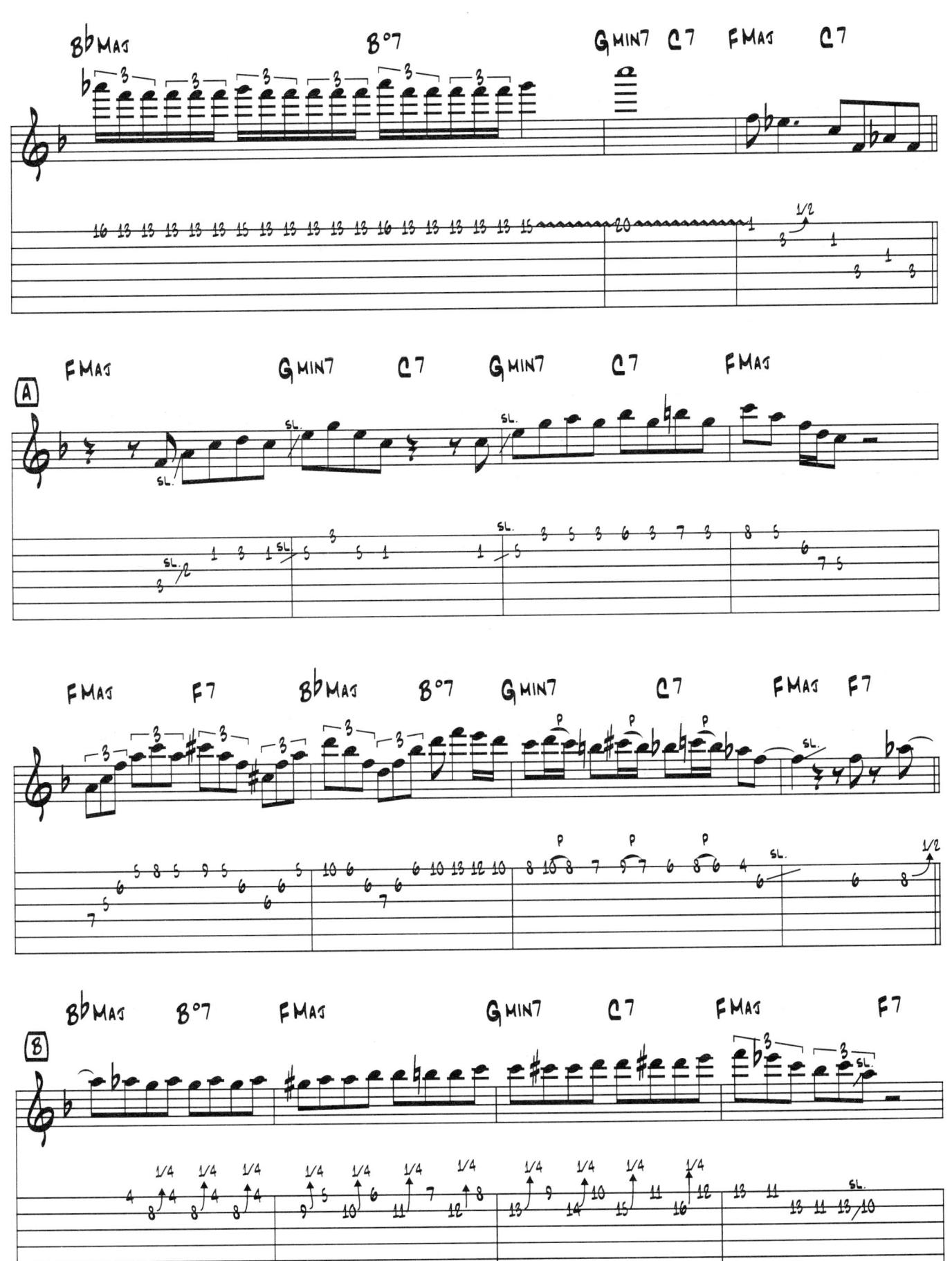

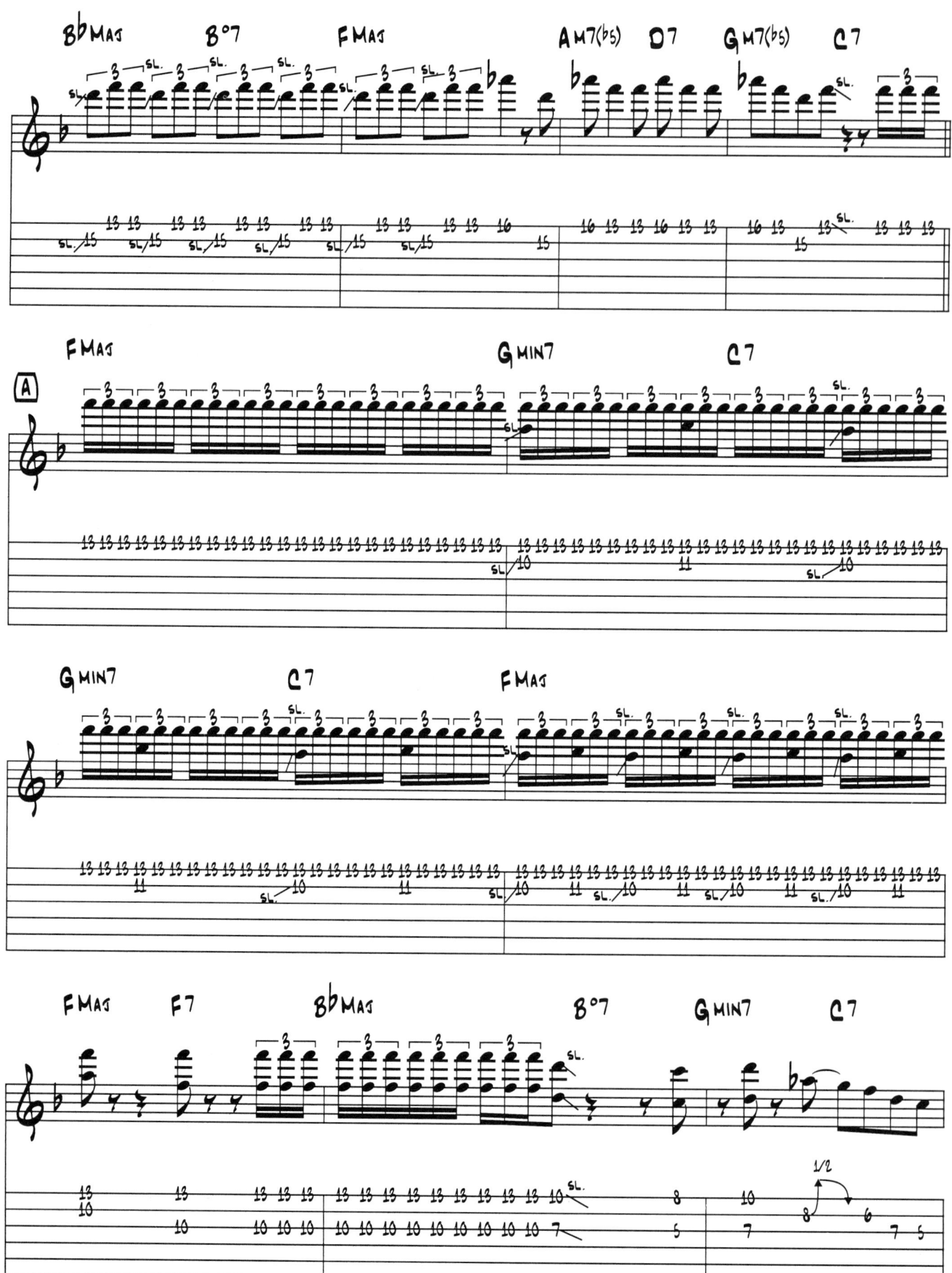

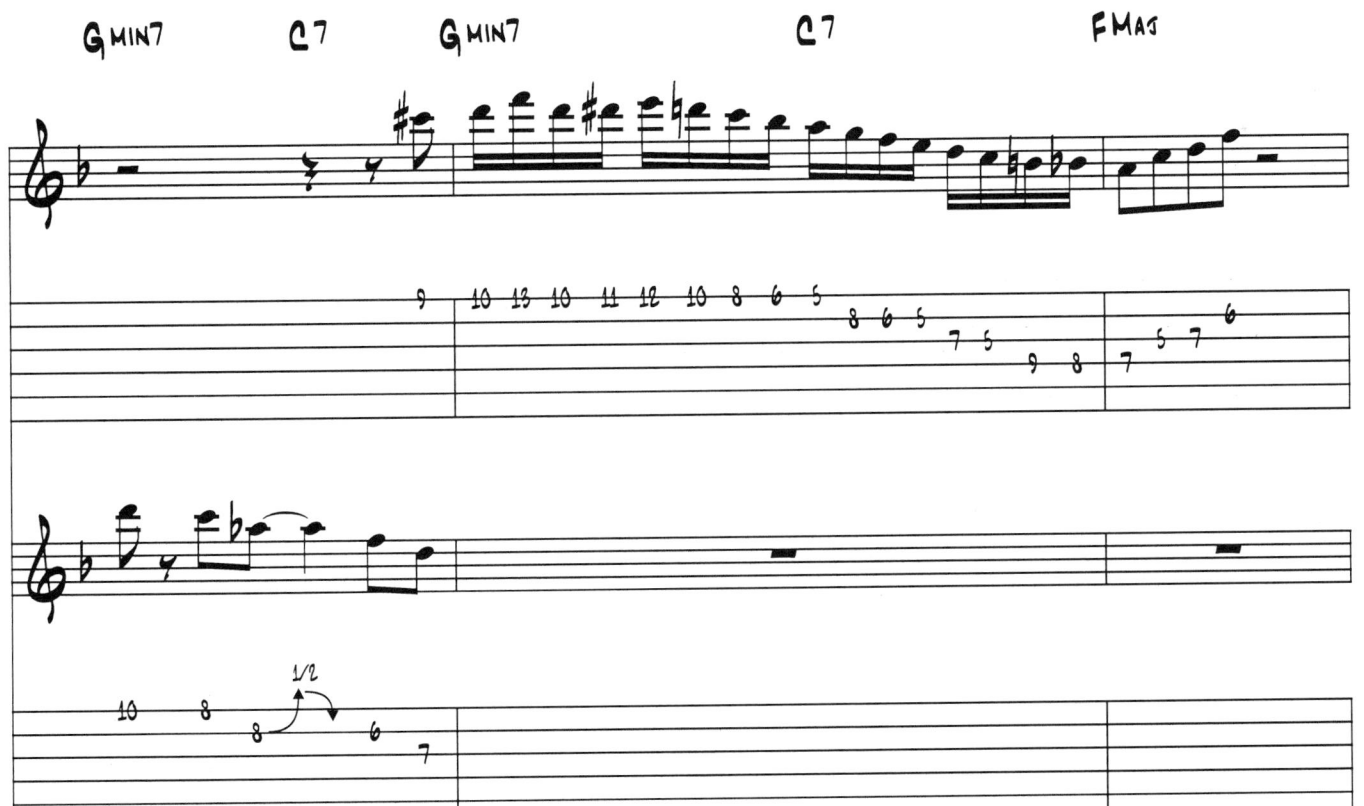

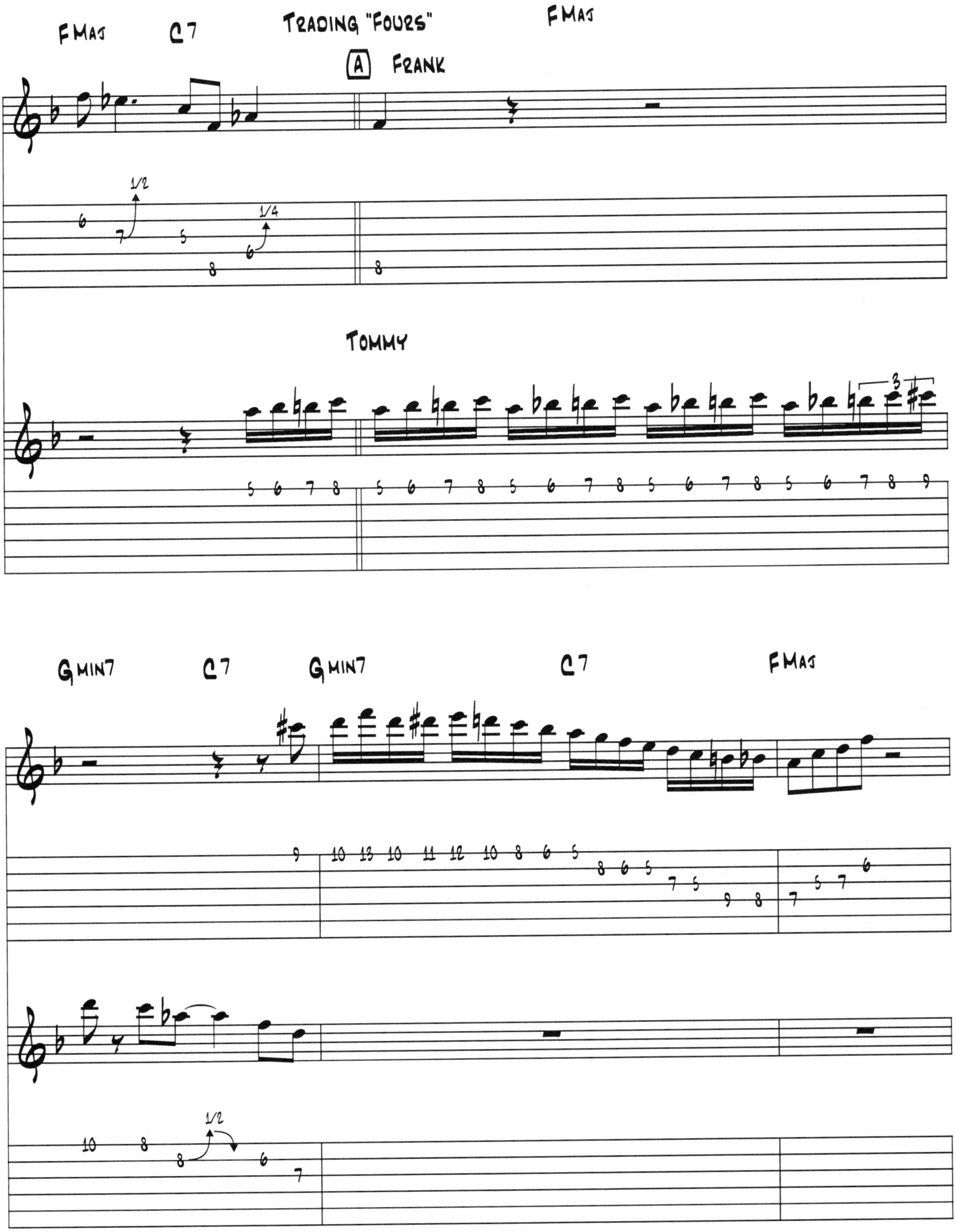
FMAJ
C7
TRADING "FOURS"
FMAJ
A FRANK
TOMMY
GMIN7
C7
GMIN7
C7
FMAJ

G MIN7
C7
F MAJ
F MAJ
F7
Bb MAJ
B°7

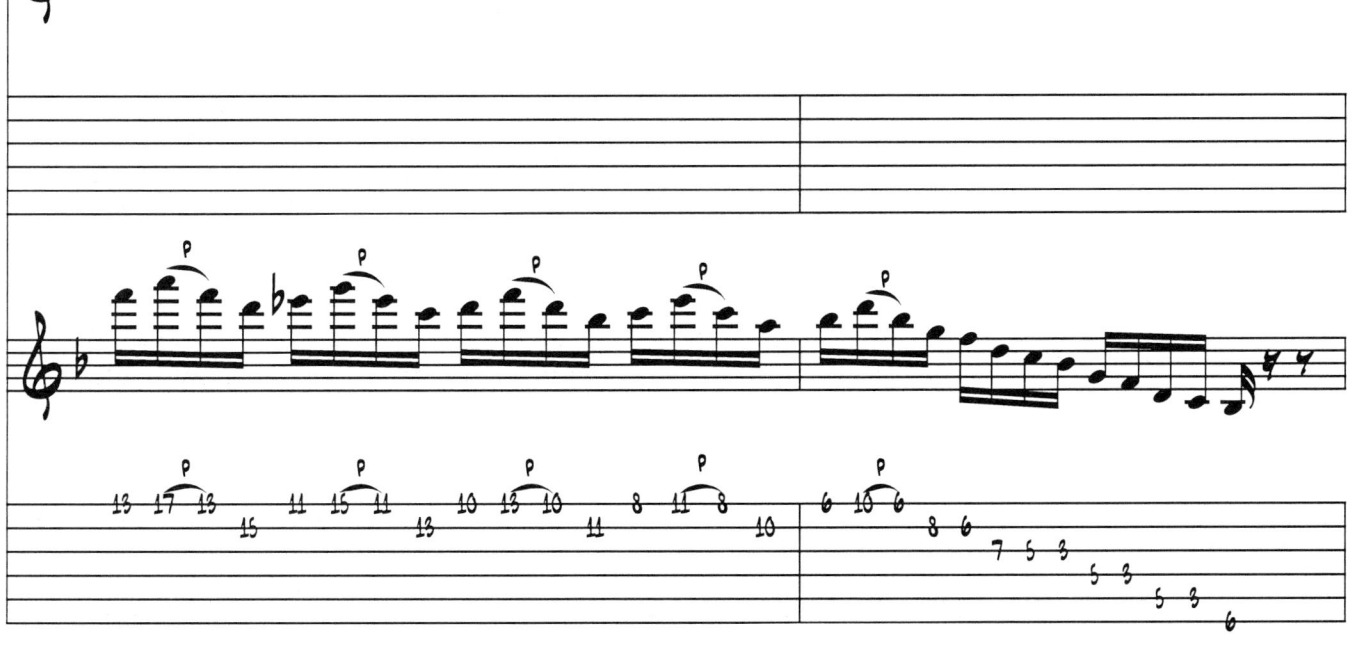

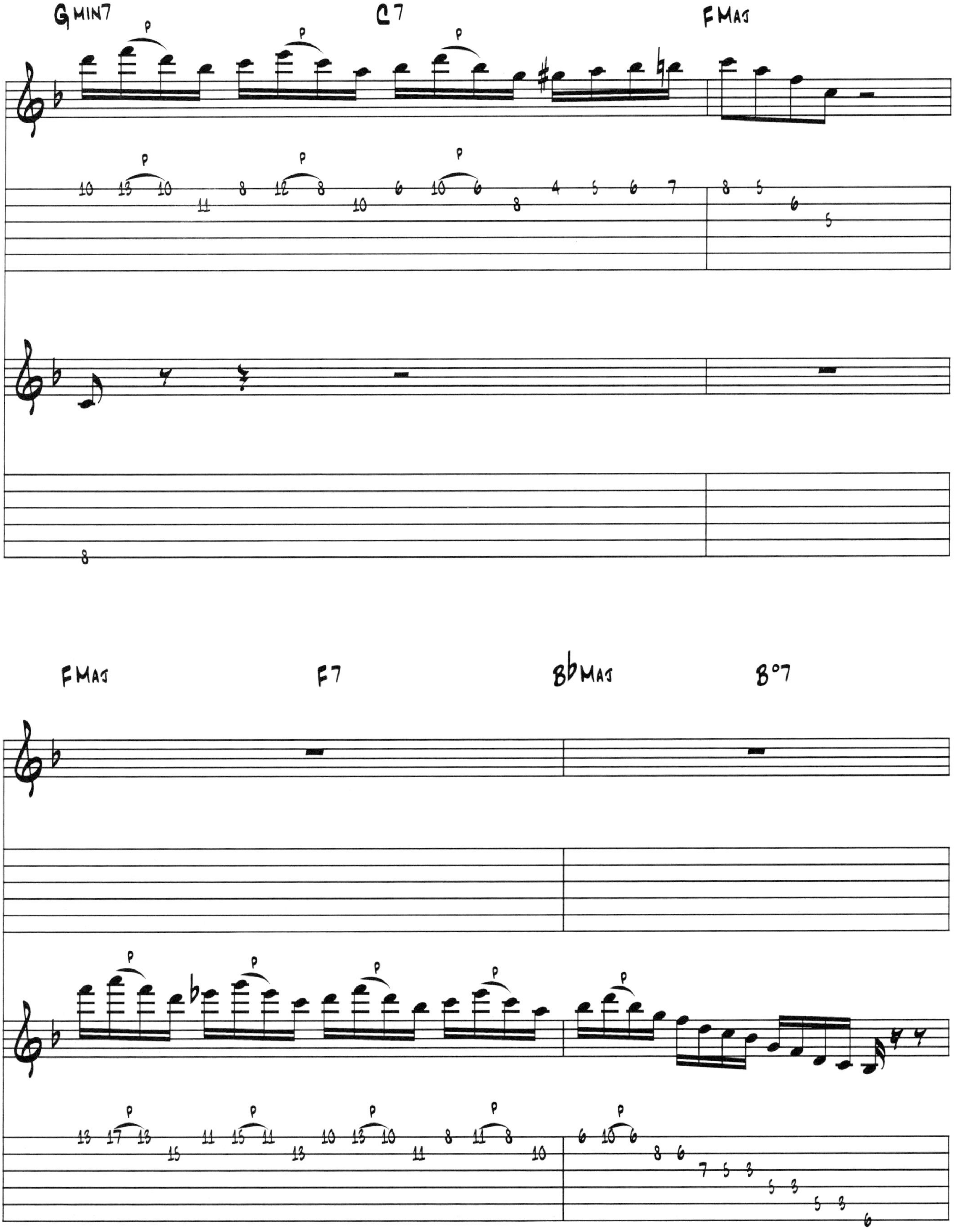

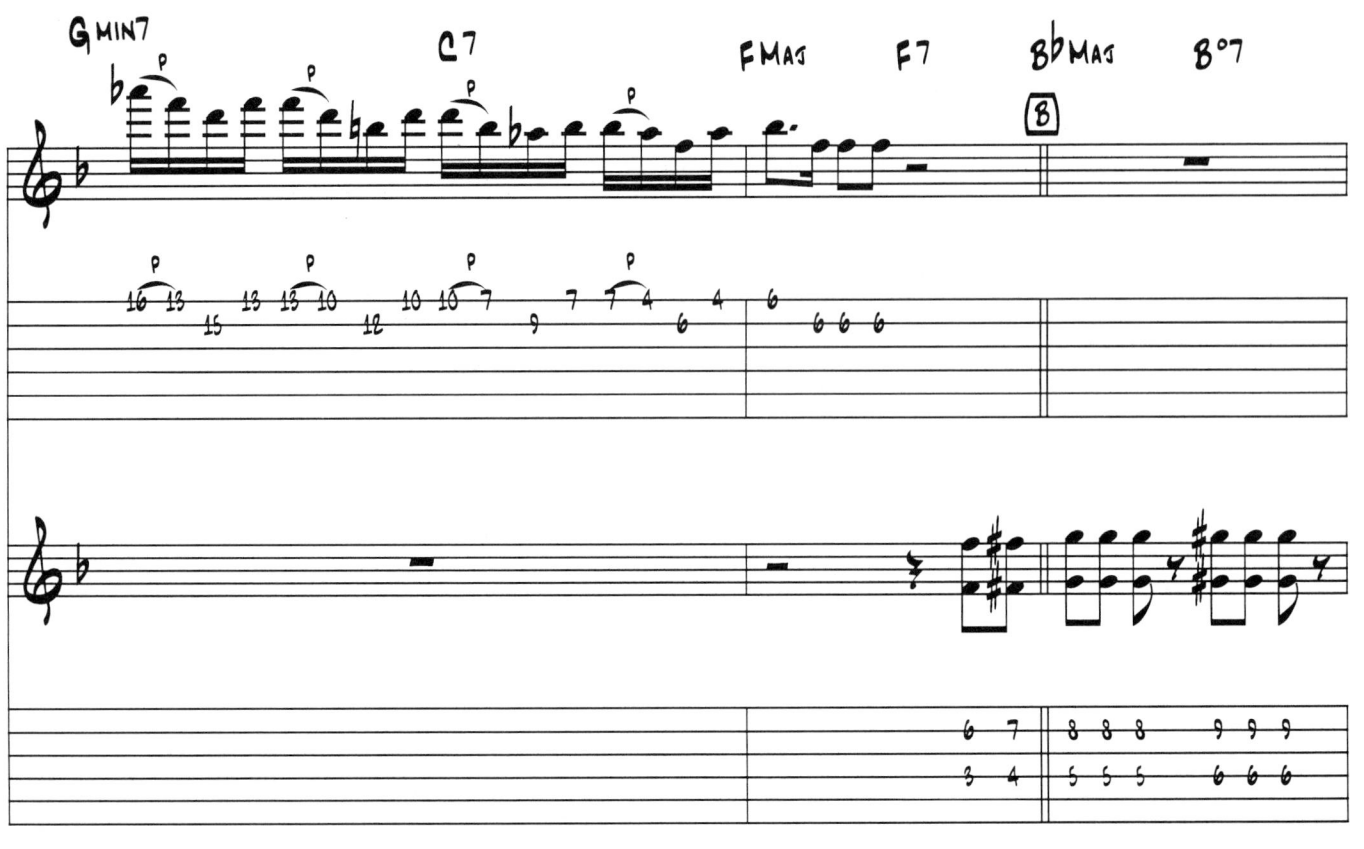
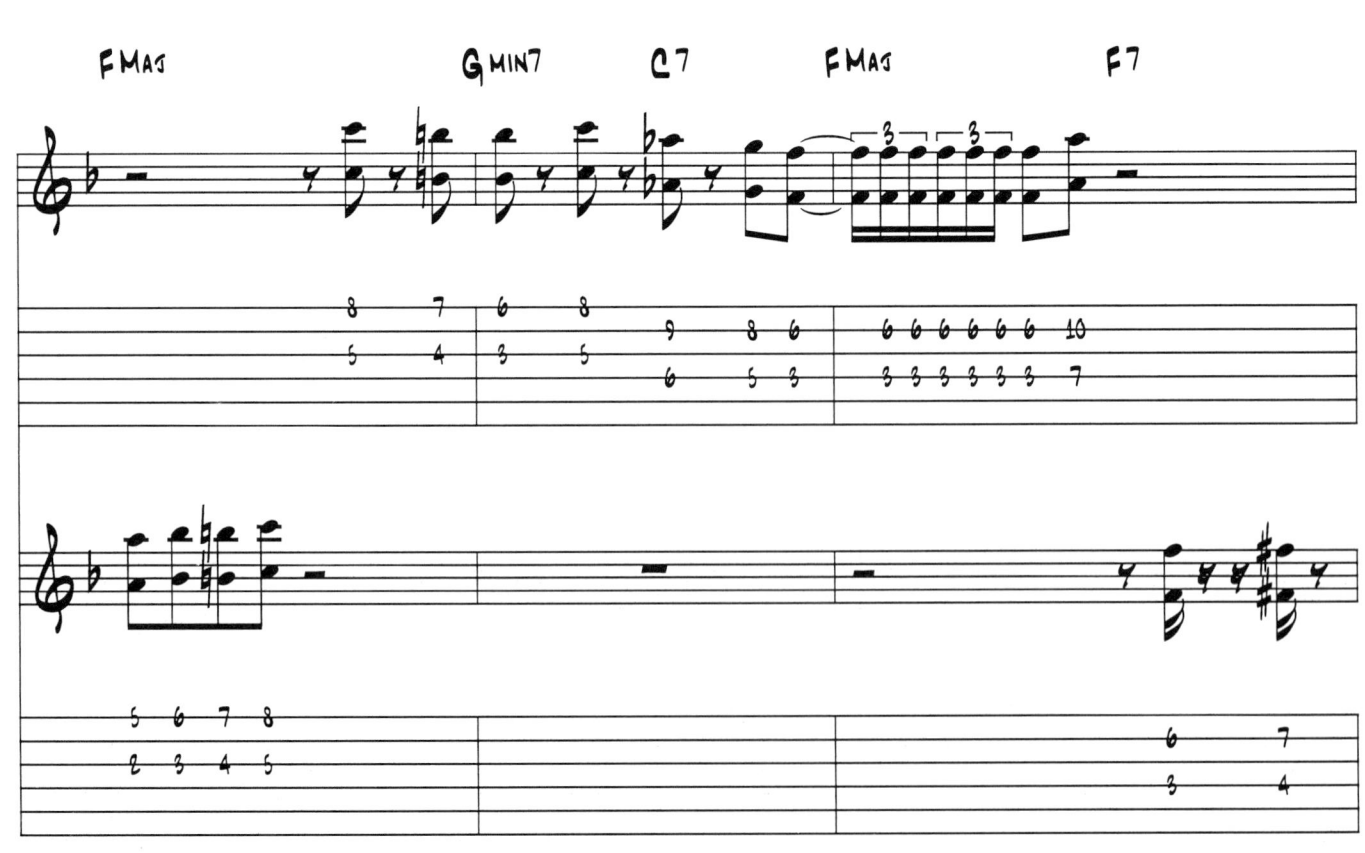

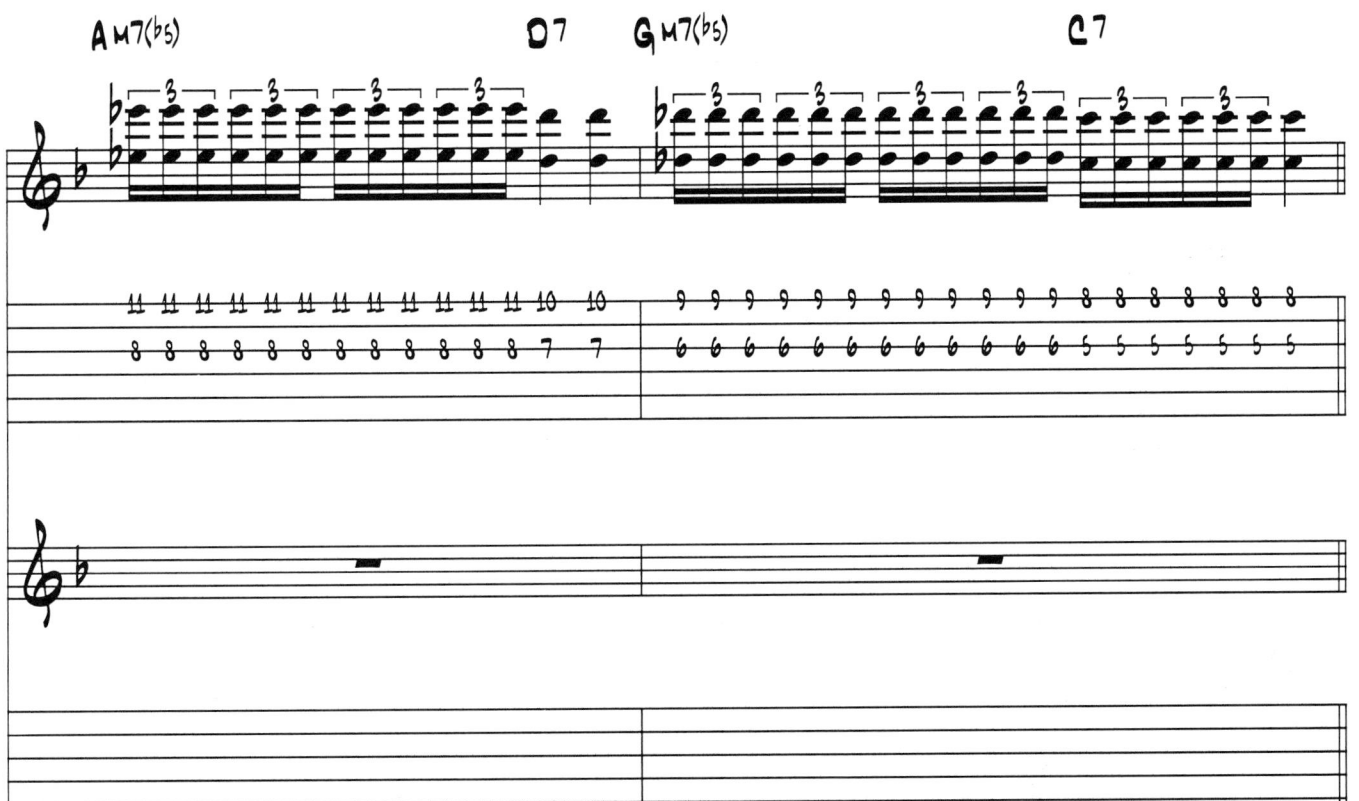

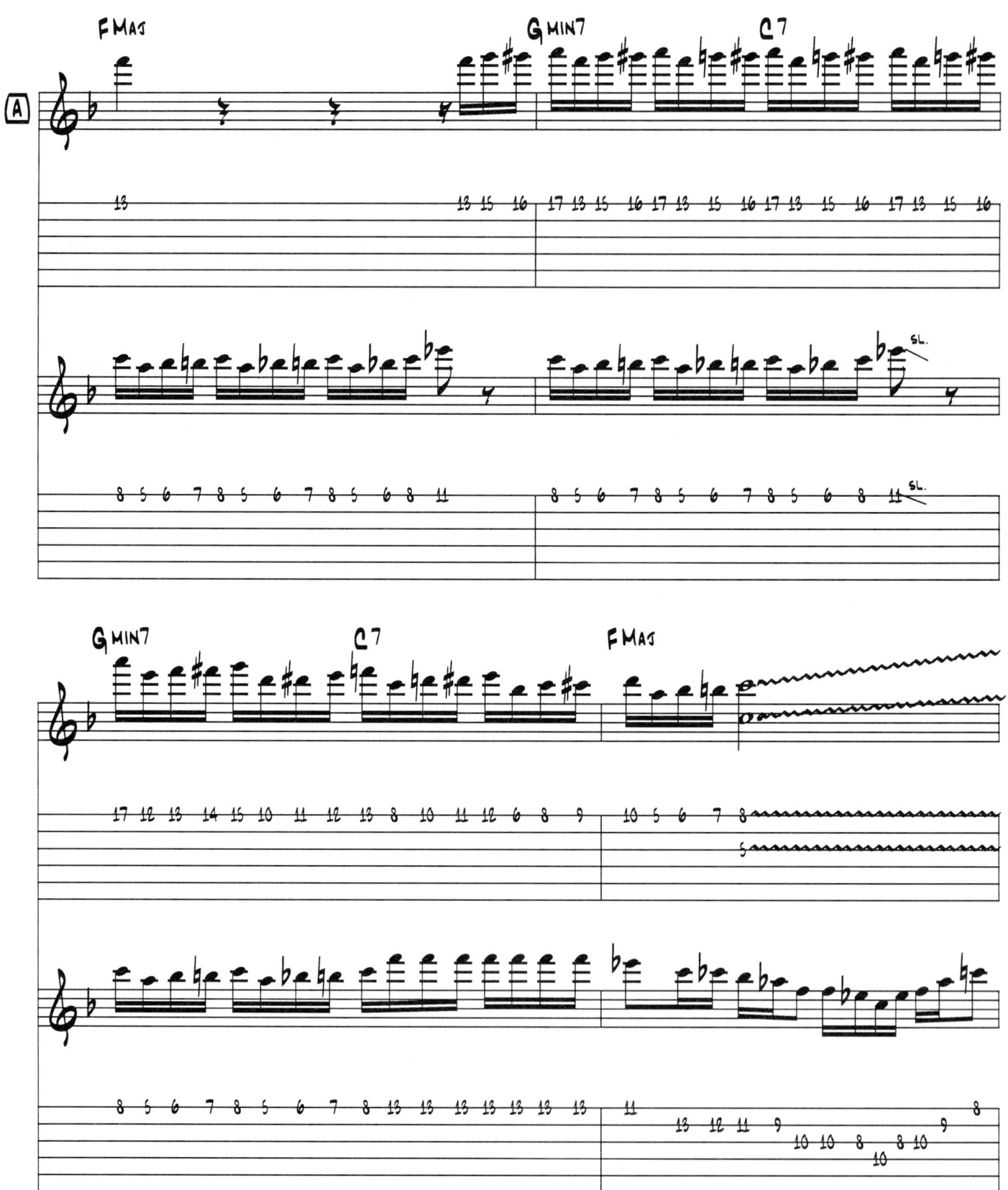

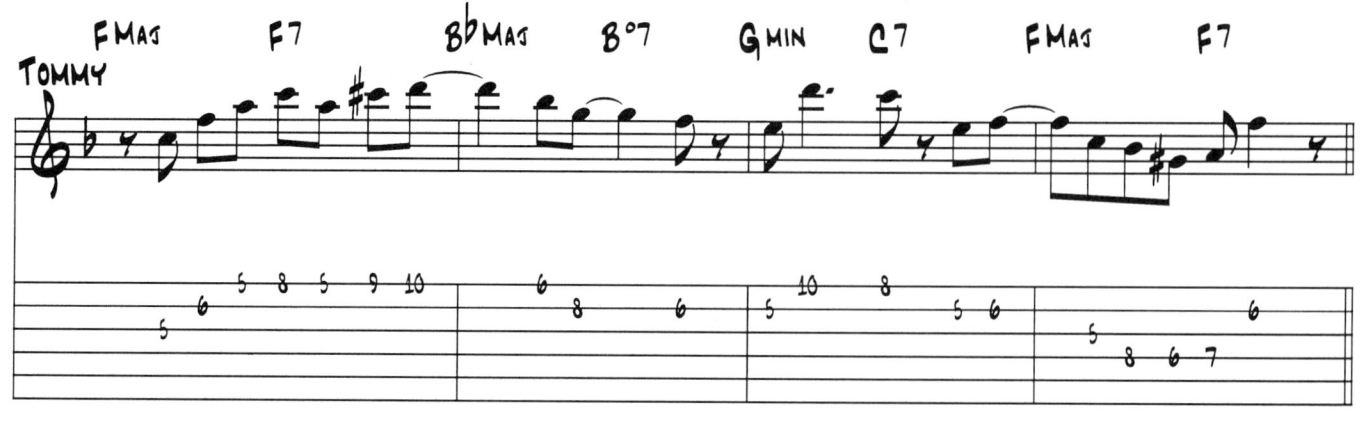
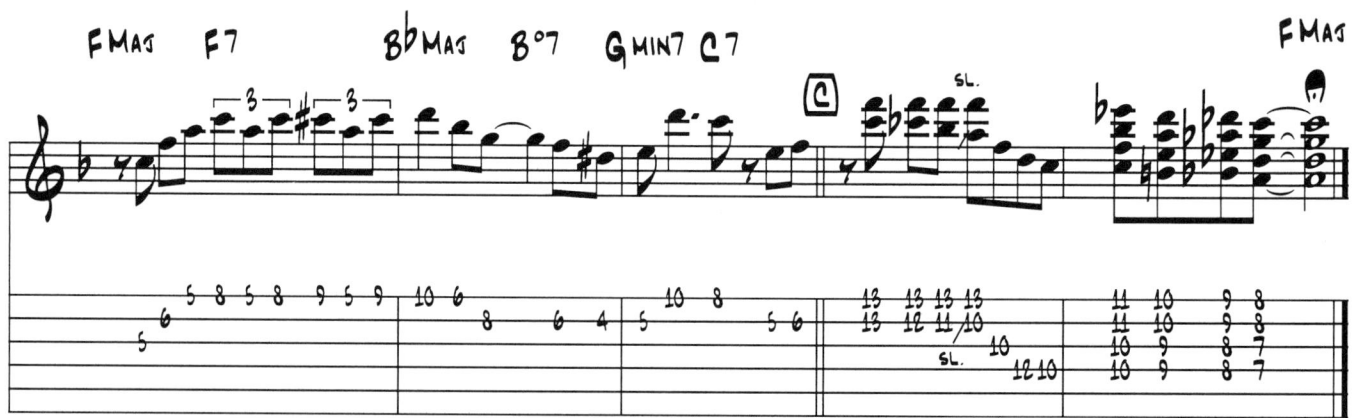
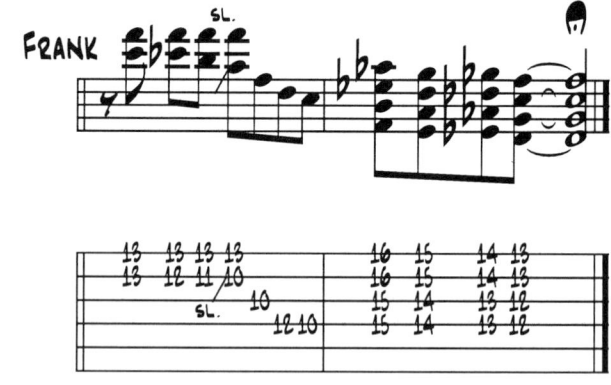

Django's Castle

Words and Music by Django Reinhardt © 1945 and 1967 (Renewed) by Publications Francis Day S. A. This Arrangement © 2010 by Publications Francis Day S.A.
All Rights in the U. S.A. and Canada Controlled by Jewel Music Publishing Co., Inc. International Copyright Secured. All Rights Reserved.
Reprinted by permission of Hal Leonard Corporation *(North America)* and Faber o.b.o. Francis Day & Hunter Ltd. *(World)*

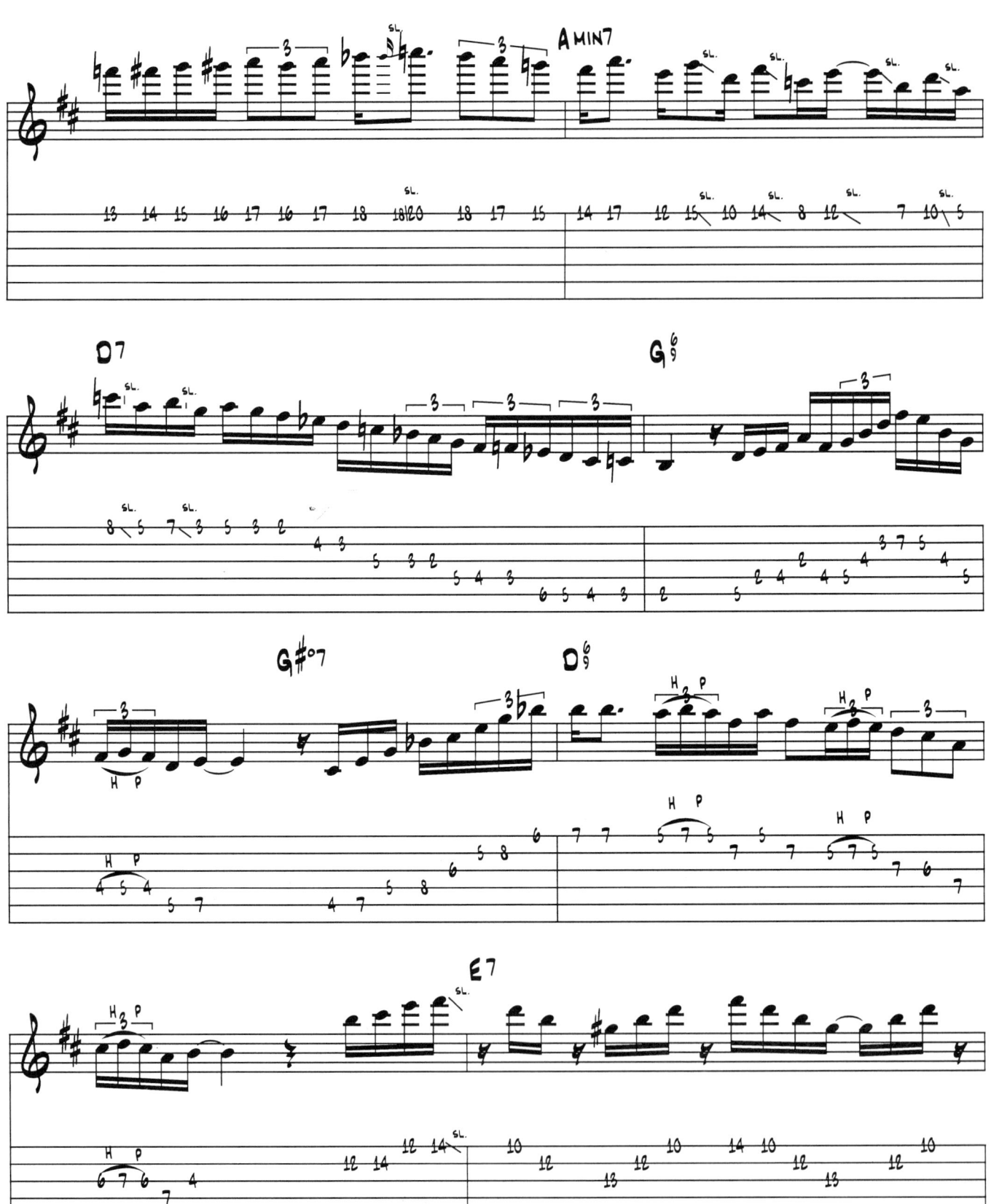

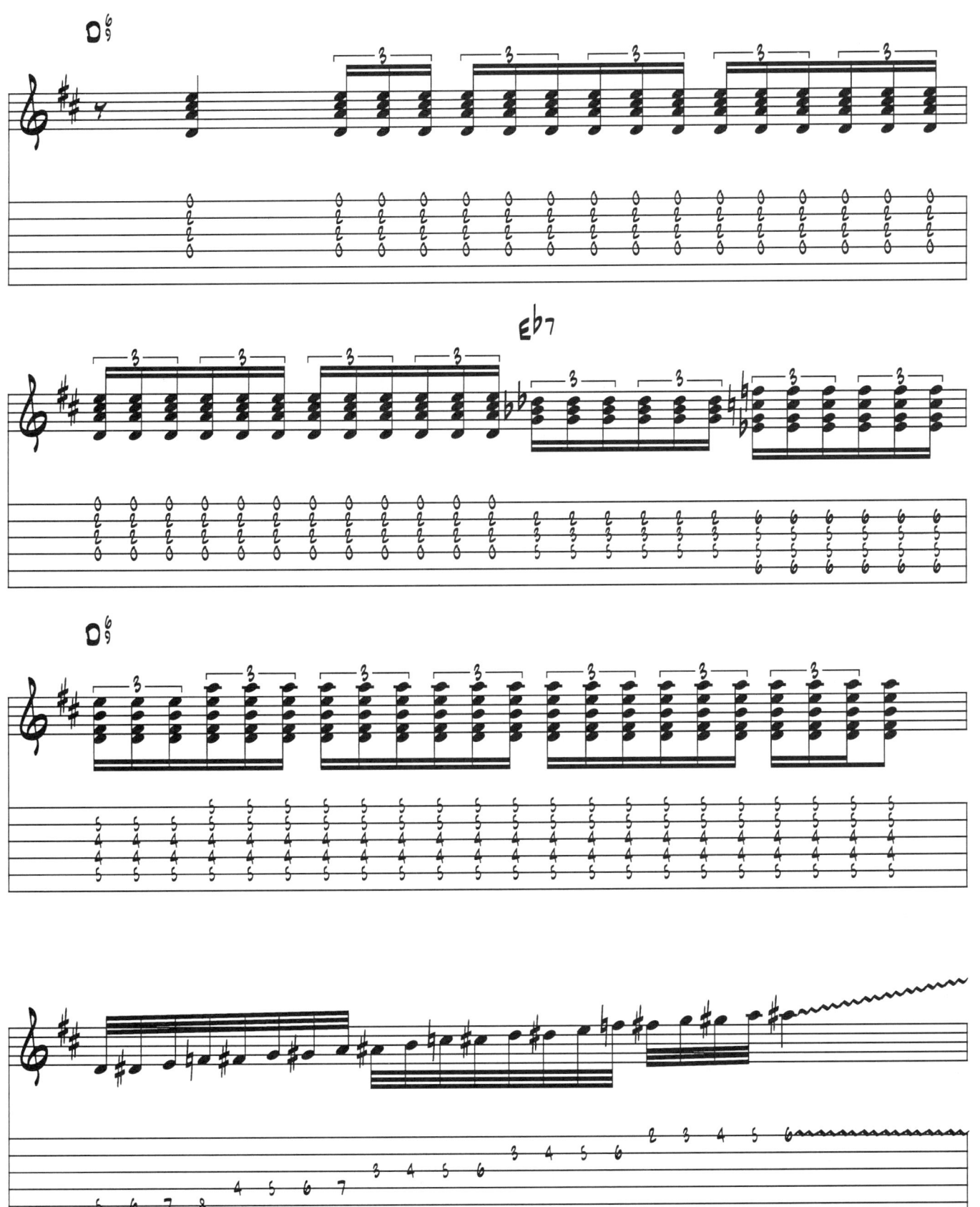

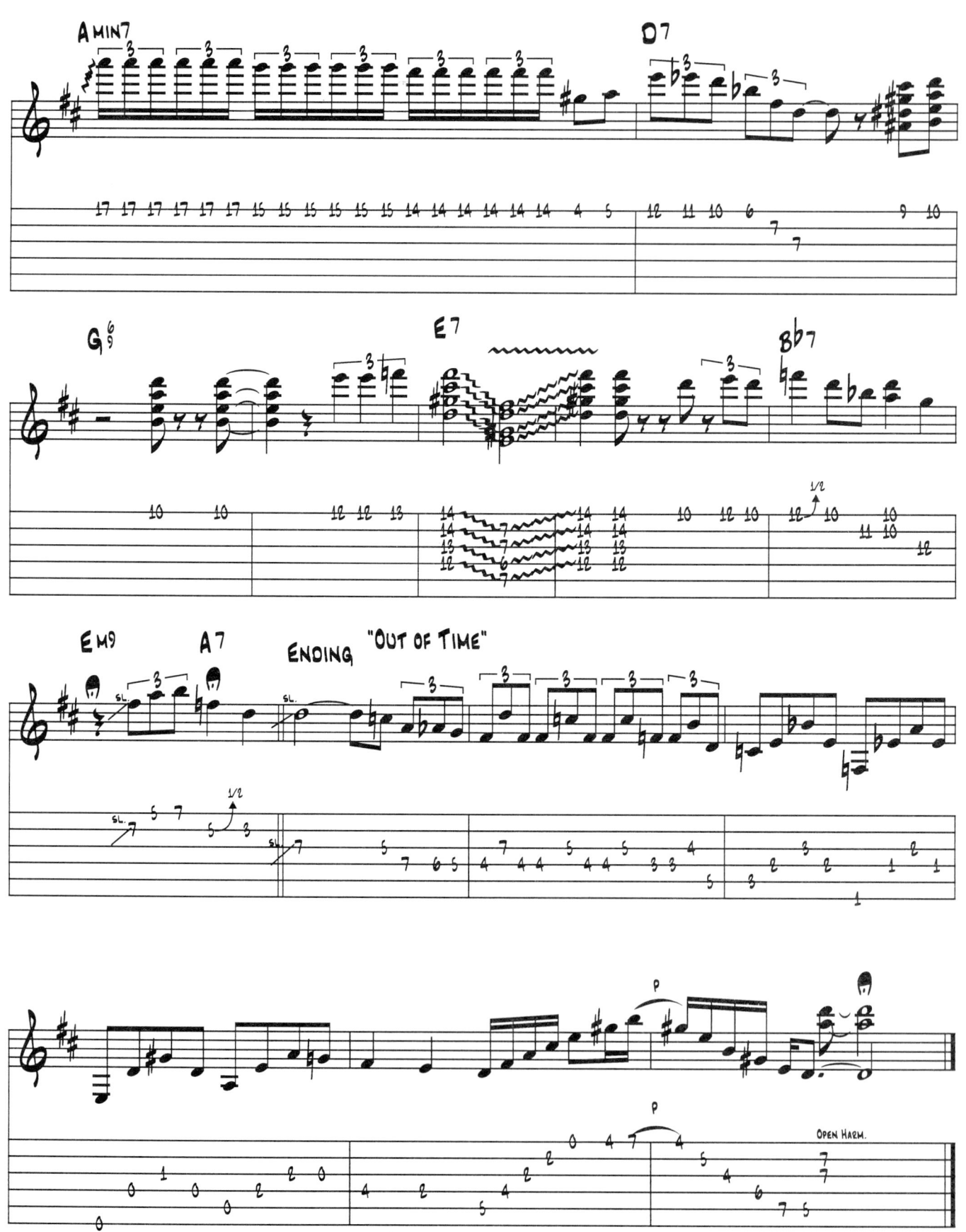

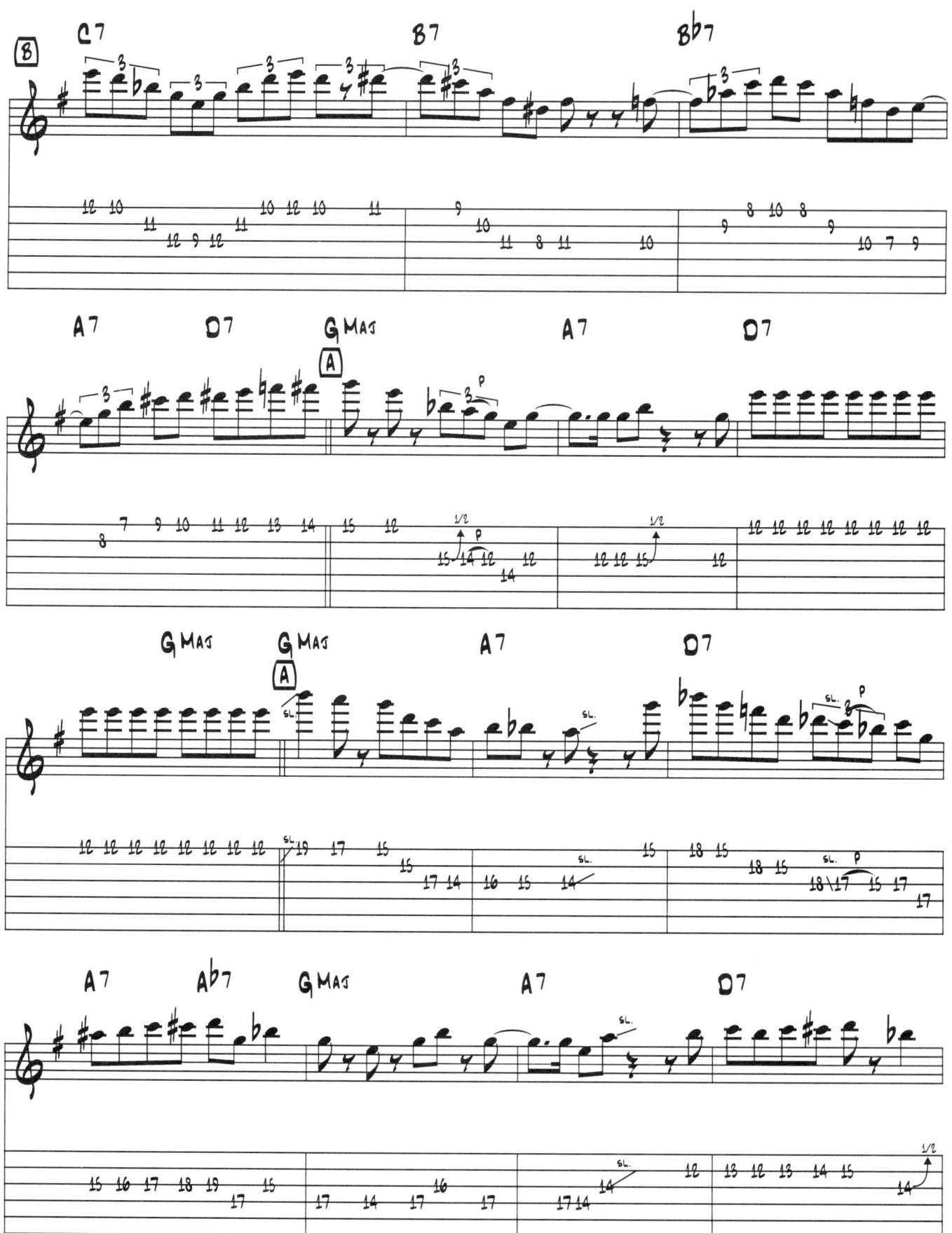

Nature Boy

Words and Music by Eden Ahbez © Golden World Enterprises. All Rights Reserved. Used by Permission.
Reprinted by permission of Golden World Enterprises *(North America)* and Faber o.b.o. Warner/Chappell *(World)*

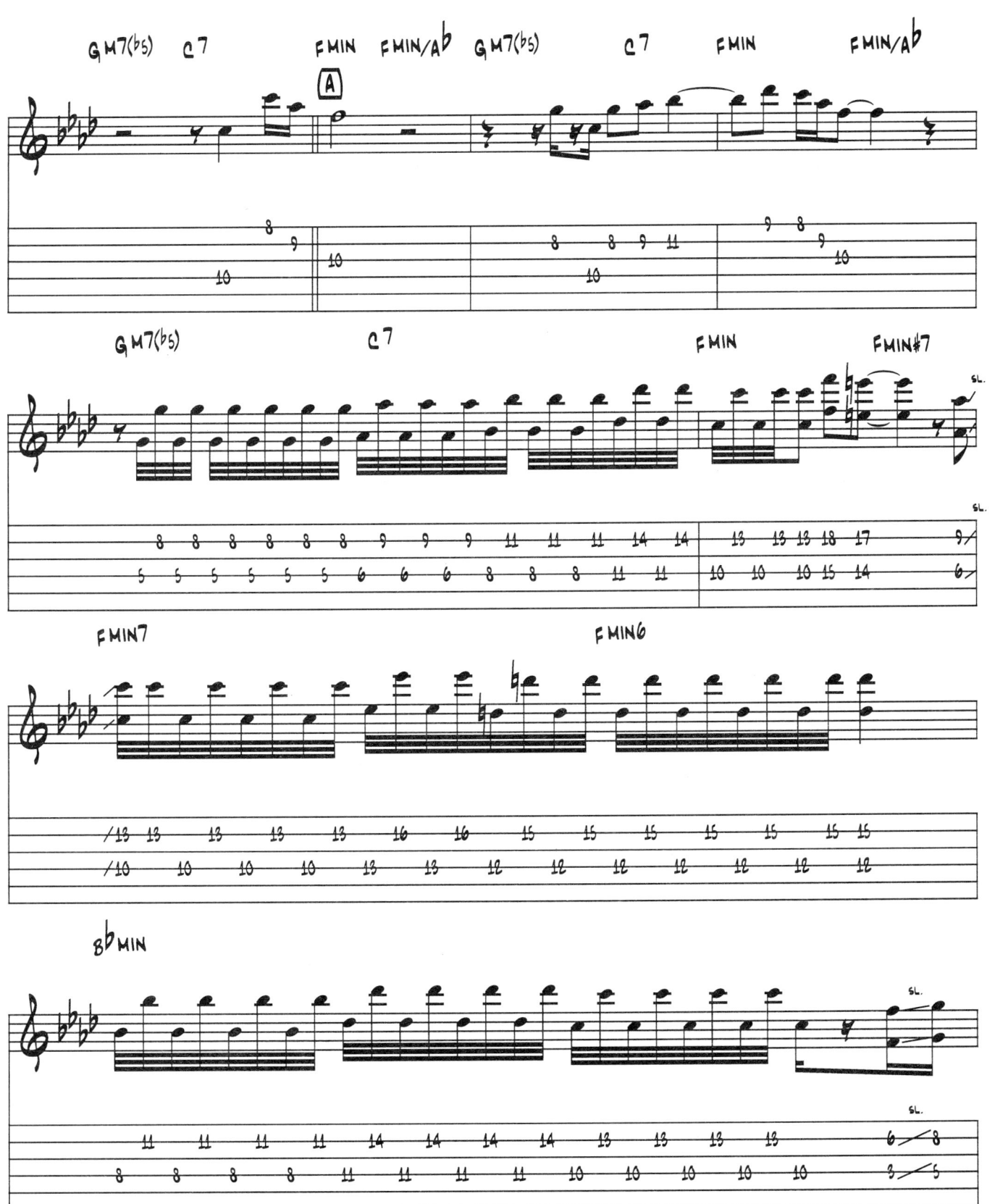

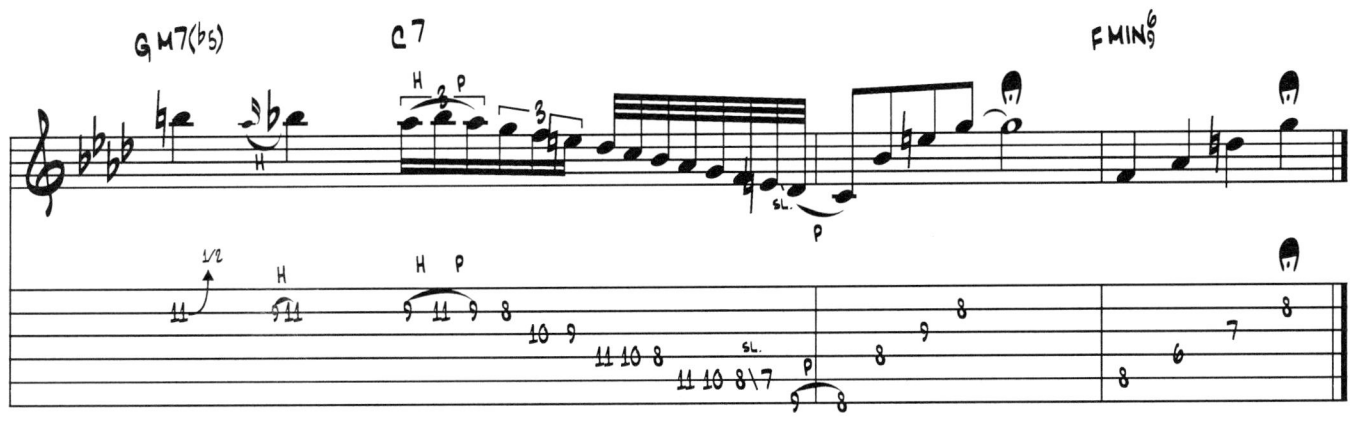

Just Us For All

Words and Music by William Emmanuel © 2009 Universal Music Publishing Pty. Ltd
This arrangement © 2010 Universal Music Publishing Pty. Ltd
All Rights in the United States and Canada Controlled and Administered by Universal-Polygram International Publishing, Inc.
All Rights Reserved. Used by Permission.
Reprinted by permission of Hal Leonard Corporation *(North America)* and of Music Sales Limited *(World)*

132

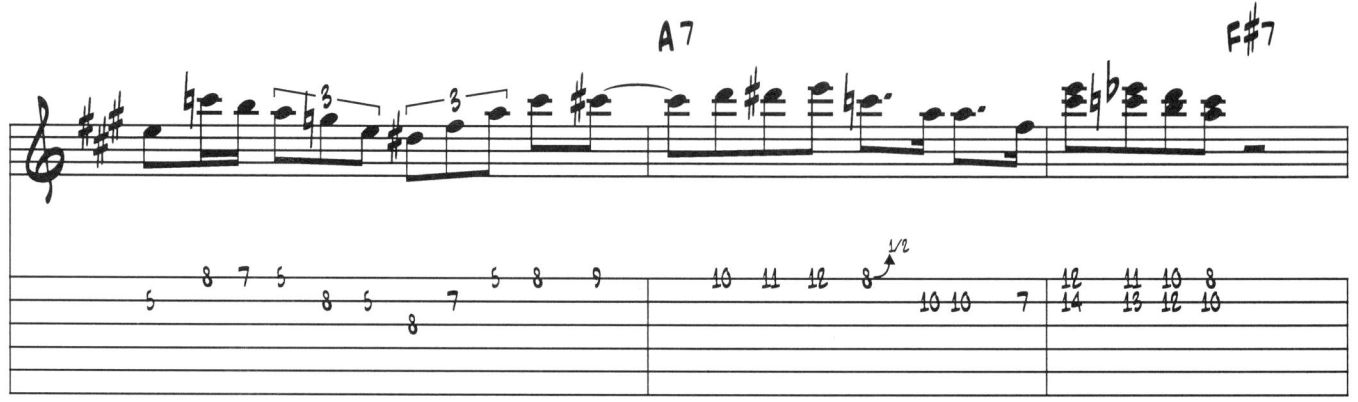

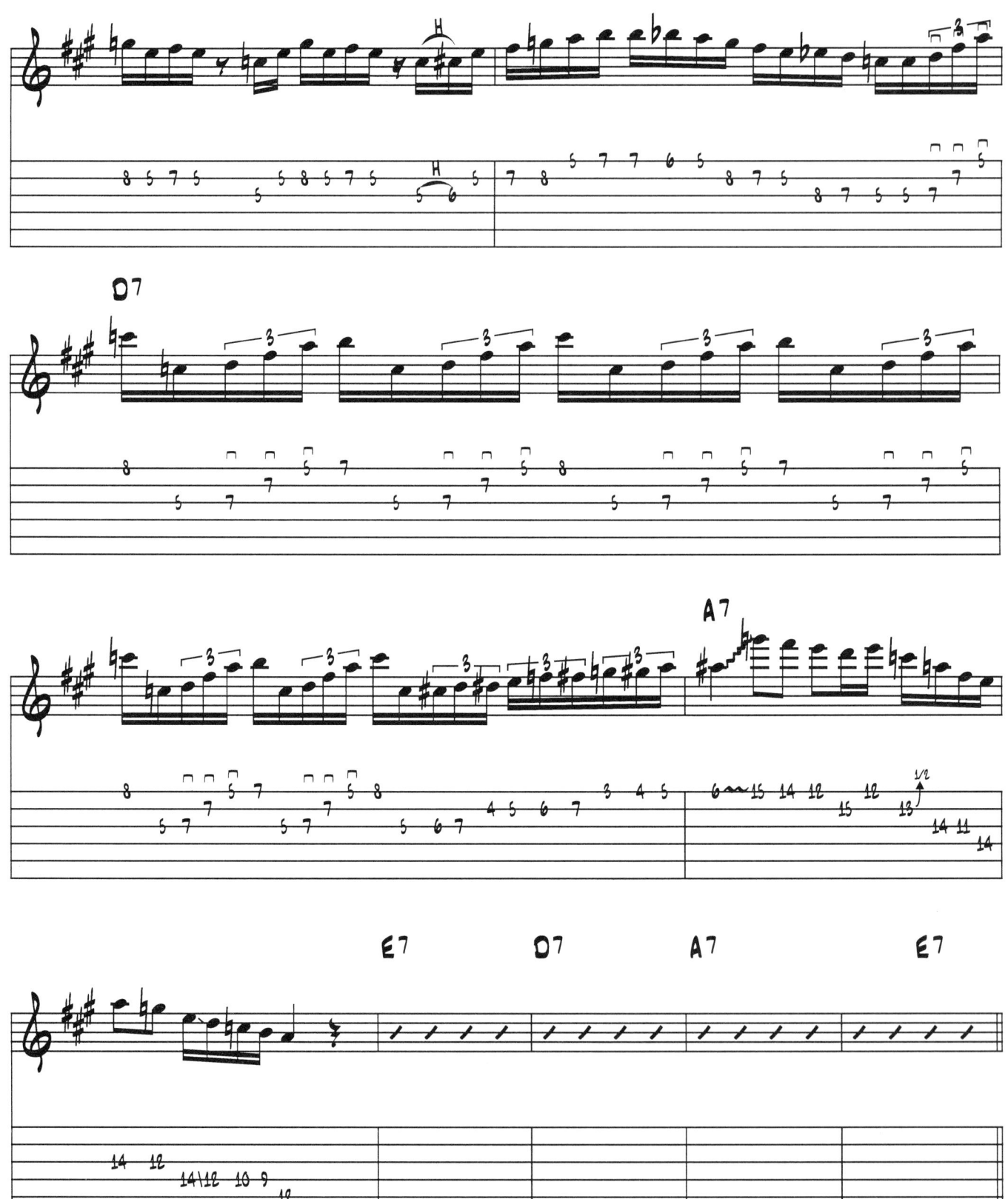

138

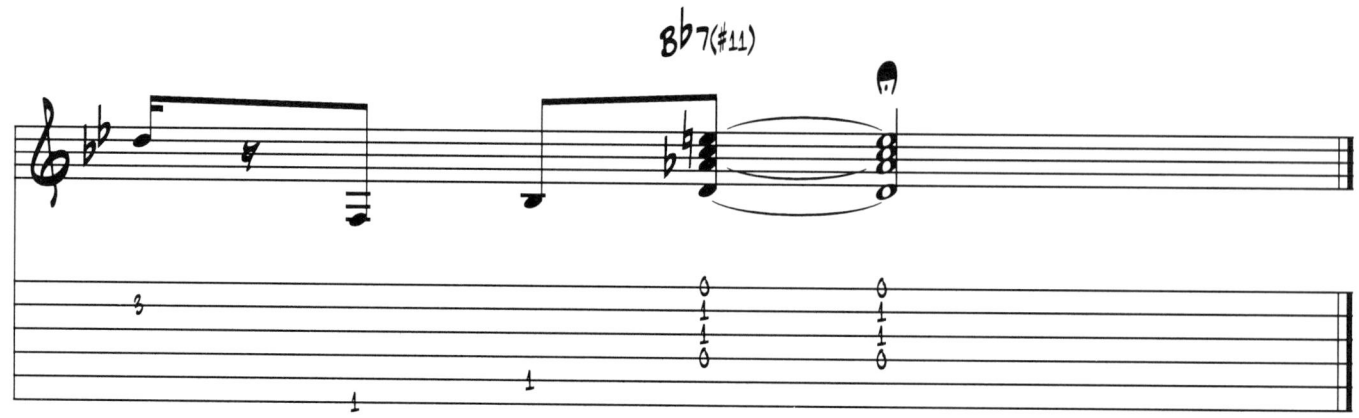